KU-736-826

Effective assessment in MFL

Ann Barnes and Marilyn Hunt

CiLT The National Centre for Languages

The views expressed in this publication are the authors' and do not necessarily represent those of CILT.

The author and publisher would like to thank copyright holders for the permission granted to reproduce copyright material, as detailed next to the relevant excerpts.

First published 2003 by CILT, the National Centre for Languages, 20 Bedfordbury, London, WC2N 4LB

Copyright © CILT 2003

Cover design: Richard Vockins

ISBN 1 904243 11 8

A catalogue record for this book is available from the British Library

All rights reserved. No part of this publication may be reproduced, stored in a retrieval system, or transmitted in any form or by any means, electronic, mechanical, photocopying, recording or otherwise without prior permission in writing from CILT or under licence from the Copyright Licensing Agency Limited, of 90 Tottenham Court Road, London W1T 4LP.

The right of Ann Barnes and Marilyn Hunt to be identified as authors of this work has been asserted by them in accordance with the Copyright, Designs and Patents Act, 1988.

Printed in Great Britain by Hobbs

CILT Publications are available from: **Central Books,** 99 Wallis Rd, London E9 5LN. Tel: 0845 458 9910. Fax: 0845 458 9912. On-line ordering: www.centralbooks.co.uk. Book trade representation (UK and Ireland): **Broadcast Book Services,** Charter House, 29a London Rd, Croydon CR0 2RE. Tel: 020 8681 8949. Fax: 020 8688 0615.

Contents

Reflection Tasks

Trainee/NQT Tasks

Head of Department Tasks

Departmental Tasks

INSET/ITE Tasks

Web templates

Acknowledgements

Many people have contributed ideas, comments and material to this book. We would like to thank everyone involved, especially:

- Mandi Collins and MFL staff at Ashlawn Bilateral School, Rugby;

- MFL Department, Cardinal Wiseman School, Coventry;

- Maria Cutler (HoD), Elly Crofton (NQT) and pupils at Coundon Court School, Coventry;

- Marianne Tchakhotine and pupils at Henley in Arden High School, Warwickshire;

- Chantal Salt, Kineton High School, Warwickshire;

- Richard Price and pupils at Polesworth High School, Warwickshire;

- Maria O'Neill, President Kennedy School, Coventry;

- Joan Hughes and pupils at Studley High School, Warwickshire;

- Jo Redford and pupils at Tile Hill Wood School and Language College, Coventry;

- All our PGCE student teachers who helped evaluate and develop the assessment materials which began this process, and who contributed some of the responses to the activities in Chapter 7;

- The members of the Subject Mentor Panel in the University of Warwick Teacher Education Partnership, whose comments and ideas were invaluable.

We are also very grateful to Emma Rees and Alan Dobson for their helpful comments on the book as it developed.

Introduction

Question: What is the point of teaching?

Answer: Pupils learning.

Question: How do we know they have learnt anything?

Answer: By assessing them.

Question: You mean in tests and exams?

Answer: That's only part of it. Assessment is ongoing; it ranges from analysing a pupil's oral answer in class and deciding what they have understood, to setting and marking end of year exams. What a teacher comments on when a pupil has handed in some homework, to a global assessment of a pupil's achievement at the end of Key Stage 3. Day-to-day evaluation of your lessons, the pupils' progress and subsequent planning of future input and activities all form part of assessment. Included in this is the essential feedback pupils need in order to progress.

The importance of assessment

It is, of course, accepted by teachers that assessment plays a vital role in successful learning. The apparently ever-growing emphasis on evidence of pupils' achievement in tests and examinations demonstrates that it is seen outside as well as within the educational context as crucial in judging the performance of both learners and teachers. But assessment is far more than the public awarding of grades or the marks recorded after class tests. It is fundamental to learners' development throughout the whole learning process. It is integral to all teachers' planning and teaching.

It may also be asserted that assessment is the area of teaching and learning where many teachers, and certainly most trainee teachers, feel less than fully confident. Assessment has been highlighted in OFSTED inspections for many years as a weak area in need of improvement (see, for example, Dobson 1998 and OFSTED 2002b). One reason for this lack of confidence and effectiveness is that the process of assessment can seem rather vague and intangible, especially at the start of a teaching career. The full meaning and potential impact of 'assessment' is not automatically understood, for example the value of feedback and the range of assessment opportunities available. It is also sometimes only considered **after** a great deal of focus on planning and teaching techniques, when it is in fact an intrinsic part of both.

 *Assessment is a means of monitoring pupils' performance, recording their progress and evaluating the effectiveness of your own teaching. It also informs your future planning and allows you to provide feedback and set targets to allow students to make further progress.* (Trainee teacher)

> *Evidence from the first round of inspections of ITE [Initial Teacher Education] providers in the late 1990s across all subjects suggests that trainees are finding the standards relating to monitoring, assessment, recording, reporting and accountability (MARRA) most challenging of all.* (Pachler and Field 2001: 26)

It is equally as challenging as a Head of Department (HoD) to ensure consistency in assessment between individual teachers and across languages. In writing this book, we are not attempting to create an extra hurdle in teaching and learning, but hoping to enable pupils and teachers to use assessment productively to improve pupils' learning, and thereby their success.

Assessment is, perhaps, not the most popular aspect of teaching and learning, precisely because it is associated with tests and examinations. Indeed, Brooks refers to assessment as the 'Cinderella aspect of teaching' (Brooks 2002: 2). To be helpful, effective and to ensure teacher sanity, assessment must be seen by teachers and learners as more than what could be regarded as a cold and negative measuring process, more than league tables, and certainly more than a simple number or letter on a page. It needs to be seen as improving the learning of pupils and their learning experience, as being useful and productive, and not as a paper exercise with no positive outcomes. For example, if used diagnostically, assessment should resemble perhaps the practice of a doctor with a patient, where an **assessment** of the patient's condition is made and, on the basis of that assessment, a decision is taken as to what to **do** next. An example in Modern Foreign Languages (MFL) might be to assess a learner's speaking by recording responses to that pupil's work on cassette: the learner becomes immediately aware of what needs to be done or revised or learnt.

 *Assessment is building up a clear and accurate picture of how a pupil is performing in order to plan future learning objectives.* (Trainee teacher)

Important work has been published recently on the value and huge potential of assessment **for** learning (as opposed to merely assessment **of** learning, which sometimes may seem to predominate) (see Brooks 2002 and particularly Black and Wiliam 1998). The Key Stage 3 National Strategy has added impetus to this development: assessment **for** learning is emphasised throughout. A renewed emphasis on **feedback**, **target setting** and therefore on **formative** assessment is beginning to be adopted enthusiastically by schools and departments. In MFL this includes using specific linguistic feedback and targets when marking pupils' work across all four Attainment Targets as well as self-assessment checklists, where pupils know what they are supposed to be learning and why, and then what they need to do to get there. Such assessment can achieve excellent results in improving pupils' learning, which then feeds through to the summative assessment of which a wider public is aware and by which pupils and teachers tend to be judged (see Chapters 5 and 6).

 *Assessment is absolutely essential for teachers to be proficient in but is possibly one of the last areas to acquire skill and aptitude in.* (Trainee teacher)

Assessment for learning is probably the most neglected topic in the whole of the educational world. (Weeden et al 2002: 150)

About this book

This book has the following aims:

- to help clarify what constitutes effective assessment in general and particularly in MFL;
- to explore aspects of assessment in MFL in a realistic and comprehensible manner and thus to be practical and usable;
- to support MFL teachers in their assessment of pupils;
- to provide throughout exemplar and discussion material and sources of ideas;
- to enable a more effective integration of monitoring and assessment into the teaching and learning process.

The book is arranged so that each chapter covers one main assessment theme, applicable to the experience of a range of readers. Within each chapter there are sections and tasks (see below) appropriate for:

- trainee teachers, many of whom may be encountering the assessment process from a teacher's perspective for the first time;
- newly qualified teachers (NQTs), who are experiencing induction into the profession;
- more experienced teachers who wish to improve their practice in assessment and need to demonstrate their effective practice, perhaps for career development;
- Heads of Department, who need to provide departmental activities or systems to create a more coherent policy and more consistent practice to promote higher standards;
- teacher trainers, who may wish to use some of the training activities with their trainees.

The tasks are categorised as follows:

- Reflection Tasks: Suitable for MFL teachers of any experience.
- Trainee/NQT tasks: Suitable particularly for trainee or newly qualified MFL teachers.
- Head of Department Tasks: Suitable for MFL teachers who are already or who intend to work as Head of Department.
- Departmental Tasks: Suitable for MFL teachers who are already or who intend to work as Head of Department.
- INSET/ITE Tasks: Suitable for Heads of Department, ITE tutors and ITE/ induction mentors.

A Head of Department from a Language College contributes a number of case studies and exemplar material throughout, and materials and quotations from a range of other teachers and trainees are used to highlight and exemplify particular issues. To help achieve the aims listed above, real examples are provided and discussed throughout and quotations from KS3 and KS4 pupils are used as appropriate to illustrate some of the issues. Further material is provided throughout the book, to be adapted as appropriate, and selected materials are included on the associated website (**www.cilt.org.uk/publications/effective assessment**) for teachers and departments to tailor to specific needs. We are not claiming by any means that the exemplar material included in the book is to be seen as a perfect model of practice; rather that it should stimulate discussion and provide starting points.

The book is intended to be used actively and when needed. For example:

- when working with trainee teachers and NQTs;
- when adapting and updating departmental policy and practice to improve performance;
- when preparing a departmental INSET;
- when analysing assessment data and designing an action plan to raise standards;
- when supporting members of staff with specific groups of pupils;
- when evaluating your own performance as an MFL teacher (perhaps for a portfolio of evidence).

Clearly, there are many MFL departments who have successful marking policies and assessment systems, and individual teachers who use feedback productively with their pupils. This book could, however, give some food for thought as to how alternatives might be considered, or current practice altered slightly. It may trigger some ideas about how a department could approach a particular issue, for example homework, or provide a topic for reflection during a training day. We include departmental tasks and activities in the chapters and provide a range of training ideas in Chapter 7.

Context of the book

Many teachers undoubtedly become frustrated when assessment advice and recommendations are rendered redundant when legislation or specifications change. This book focuses on assessment **principles**, which form the basis of effective teaching and learning. Current examination specifications and National Curriculum details provide a framework around the assessment principles. Of course, National Curriculum and GCSE are central to the context in which assessment is undertaken and the book pays considerable attention to these areas, but the underlying assessment practices and ideas will apply whatever legislation or examination system is in place.

The book has been developed from work carried out by university MFL Subject Tutors with MFL teachers, Heads of Department, Subject Mentors in schools and MFL teacher trainees. They have contributed extensively to the ideas and examples, and provided valuable feedback on its aims and content.

Assessment – introductory thoughts and definitions

> ## Constant examining demotivates low-achievers
>
> *TES* 28.6.02

> ## More than a year swallowed up by exam agenda
>
> *TES* 12.7.02

The impression might be gained from newspaper headlines and other media reports that assessment is focused entirely on measuring achievement. This is undoubtedly important, it forms a crucial record of learners' progress and is a part of the accountability mentioned previously. But emphasis solely on summative assessment runs the risk of neglecting assessment for learning – the vital feedback and developmental process involved in learning. On different occasions and for different audiences, different forms of assessment are appropriate. It is very important that a pupil's overall achievement in a language is measured and recorded by means of an external examination at the age of 16. The certificate and grade **summarise** what the pupil has attained. However, such a form of assessment does not necessarily move the learner on in his or her learning of the language, even though it may gain him or her entry to an advanced course. Effective **formative** assessment should, of course, make a major contribution to improvements in achievement in summative assessment.

Broadfoot (2000) makes us aware of the necessary **human** element in effective assessment, i.e. assessment **for** learning. She notes that where there is an over-emphasis on summative, measurable assessment, there is the danger of neglecting any other kind and ending up with: 'A world in which what cannot be measured in a systematic way is deemed not to exist.' (Broadfoot 2000: 199)

She states that there are three main arguments:

1 *There is now overwhelming evidence that we collectively pay a high educational and social price for an obsession with measurement.*

2 *The emphasis on a 'measurement driven' pursuit of higher standards that has characterised educational policy has not been successful in raising overall standards of student achievement.*

3 *Obsession with the pursuit of 'objective' measurement has constrained education to a point where fundamentally important, but necessarily more amorphous, forms of learning are becoming excluded.*

(Broadfoot 2000: 200)

Although Broadfoot uses the term 'amorphous', which may sound rather negative, the idea of formative assessment as being more difficult to record or display as a number is certainly true.

From this perspective, assessment needs to fulfil more than the 'obvious' function of measurement. It should measure **what** is necessary and appropriate **when** it is necessary and appropriate. Recording figures and statistics for the sake of doing so wastes time and diverts energy from guiding learners in their learning.

Assessment can feel very intimidating or frightening from the learner's perspective. Indeed, it may even be used as a threat (albeit disguised). Much has been written on examination stress. Yet effective learning requires effective assessment: from a teacher, from oneself, from peers. Without assessment, how does a learner become aware of progress or how to improve? Assessment could therefore be seen in two ways, as both Broadfoot and Brooks point out.

> *Assessment is a powerful tool for good or ill; used in ill thought-out ways it condemns those in its power to the at best mechanistic, at worst fruitless, pursuit of arbitrary goals. Against this, it can be the key to releasing the measure of individual engagement that could transform many different aspects of our society.* (Broadfoot 2000: 215)

> *Two key ideas:*
> * *The dual potential of assessment to enhance or inhibit meaningful learning*
> * *Assessment can be both a tool for teaching and a straitjacket restricting it.*
> (Brooks 2002: 11)

One danger of assessment, often mentioned by teachers, is that everything becomes assessment-driven. It is probably **summative** assessment which is alluded to, i.e. a concentration on final examinations or on end of Key Stage 3 assessment. If the term 'assessment-driven' is viewed from a different perspective, it can be seen very positively. In this case it would describe a process in which learning is assessed constructively and used to move forward. Learning is not assumed just to happen. Merely because learners have been exposed to language and have written something down, it is not assumed they have understood. Likewise, marks recorded in mark books can appear very impressive and give the appearance that the teacher is informed about learners' progress. But unless the marks are clearly understood and flagged then they may as well not be there.

Conclusion

This book aims to help teachers, at whatever stage in their careers, ensure that their assessment practices improve pupils' learning of Modern Foreign Languages. In this way, assessment can be viewed positively by both teacher and learner, rather than as something of doubtful value or as an incursion into precious time. Learning should not be driven by assessment but should flourish through using assessment well.

1

What is assessment?

As illustrated in the introduction, assessment certainly remains the focus of a great deal of local and national attention, with debate around standards, external examinations, national tests and international comparisons. In such a climate, it could be easy to lose sight of the every day nature of assessment, i.e. the interaction between teachers and pupils about their learning and how to improve it. In Modern Foreign Languages this is the continuous process of evaluation which takes place, for example, while an oral whole-class presentation of new language is in progress and the teacher assesses how much more practice is needed, which pupils are participating more successfully than others, whether elements need to be revisited from previous work, etc. The diagram below illustrates how differently assessment tends to be viewed depending on the context. Assessment activity can take place at any point on this spectrum, according to the extent to which it is primarily formative or summative, for example.

The assessment spectrum

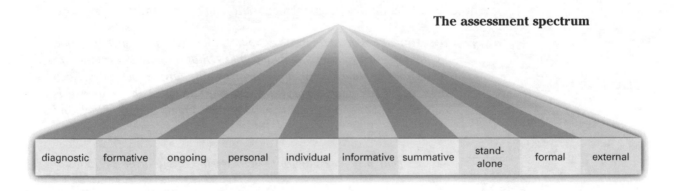

| diagnostic | formative | ongoing | personal | individual | informative | summative | stand-alone | formal | external |

National tests would be placed on the right-hand side of the assessment spectrum (shown above), and feedback to pupils on the left.

There is certainly a role in teaching and learning for both ends of the assessment spectrum – the **personal, individual** assessment where learners receive feedback on their progress, alongside the **formal, often external** assessment to provide measurement data. By assessing and feeding back to learners in the classroom at the left-hand side of the spectrum, performance in the more formal assessment tests at the right-hand side should benefit, and some summative tests themselves can provide the stimulus for further individual progress if used constructively.

The recent influential work on assessment **for** learning (see for example the work of the Assessment Reform Group 2002) has led to formative assessment being subject to scrutiny and, as with any current focus, there is perhaps a danger that only the more obvious elements may be implemented and some essential parts neglected. It must also be remembered that effective, targeted formative assessment is more likely to lead to success in summative tests and examinations. Formative assessment is certainly not just about creating a more productive classroom-based atmosphere: it should mean improved results. Good teachers have always assessed formatively and reacted to assessment 'results': the current focus highlights how this process can be carried out to best effect.

This chapter will look at the various forms assessment takes and how they link together. Whatever you assess needs to be what is **useful** to the pupils' current learning and future progress.

What exactly is assessment?

There are many reasons for assessing, although the ultimate aim of all these is the improvement of pupils' learning.

Assessment can:

- help pupils see their progress;
- indicate to teachers and learners what needs to be worked on (and help with their planning);
- contribute to decisions regarding which learners should be in which sets/take which language(s)/study a language further/be given extra support, etc;
- help set individual, group, departmental and school targets;
- enable others (e.g. parents, senior management) to be aware of learners' progress;
- give precise information to learners on what they need to do to improve.

Three useful definitions of assessment help clarify the issues:

> **1** *Assessment: refers to all those activities undertaken by teachers – and by the students in assessing themselves – that provide information to be used as feedback to modify teaching and learning activities. Such assessment becomes **formative assessment** when the evidence is actually used to adapt the teaching to meet student needs. (Black and Wiliam 1998)*

> **2** *'Assessment provides underpinning for effective learning.' (Dobson 2002: 6)*

> **3** ***Assessment for learning** is the process of seeking and interpreting evidence for use by learners and their teachers to decide where the learners are in their learning, where they need to go and how best to get there. (The Assessment Reform Group 2002)*

Assessment encompasses, then, all aspects of the teaching and learning process. In MFL, this could be something as straightforward as a whole-class starter activity on numbers to ensure learners understand and are able to produce them before moving on to telling the time. It is also a part of, for example, building up more complex sentences at the end of Key Stage 3 and Key

Stage 4, and working with learners to map out exactly what they need in order to do this and how; which elements they feel confident with and how they can expand on them. Individually, one example of helping learners at all levels improve their achievement and take their learning forward is by developing with them an interactive checklist. This is stuck in the front of a pupil's book or file: it is individual to the pupil and changes as he or she improves. When a pupil fills an exercise book or starts a new file, the personalised checklist goes with him or her. (See also Barnes 1999: 267.)

Perhaps it is also useful at this point to look at what assessment is **not,** or, at least, what it **should not** be:

- There is no point assessing if it has no effect on pupils' learning or achievements.
- Perfect records of marks are meaningless if they are not used effectively.

Many of the prejudices or concerns teachers may have about assessment revolve around this interpretation of assessment, i.e. as bureaucracy or burden. Pupils may of course also perceive it as an additional, stressful problem.

> *Tests in MFL are boring, they put me under pressure and make me nervous.* (Boy, Year 8)

Stobart and Gipps (1997) refer to assessment **of** learning as having **managerial** purposes and assessment **for** learning as having **professional** purposes, i.e. essentially formative. Both types of assessment should have the improvement of learning as their goal. Managerial purposes are looked at in more detail in Chapter 6, and professional purposes in Chapter 4.

Monitoring, assessment, recording, reporting and accountability (MARRA)

Until recently the acronym MARRA was used in relation to assessment. In order to work out exactly what is involved in assessment, it is helpful to look at the elements of the acronym used.

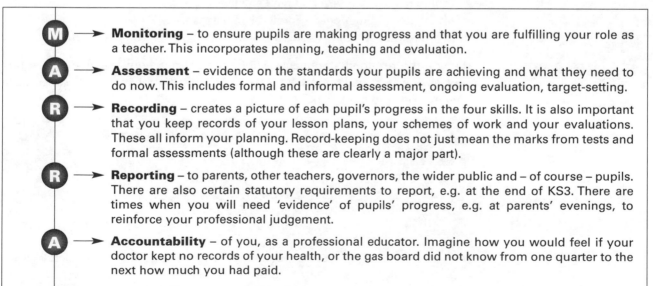

M → **Monitoring** – to ensure pupils are making progress and that you are fulfilling your role as a teacher. This incorporates planning, teaching and evaluation.

A → **Assessment** – evidence on the standards your pupils are achieving and what they need to do now. This includes formal and informal assessment, ongoing evaluation, target-setting.

R → **Recording** – creates a picture of each pupil's progress in the four skills. It is also important that you keep records of your lesson plans, your schemes of work and your evaluations. These all inform your planning. Record-keeping does not just mean the marks from tests and formal assessments (although these are clearly a major part).

R → **Reporting** – to parents, other teachers, governors, the wider public and – of course – pupils. There are also certain statutory requirements to report, e.g. at the end of KS3. There are times when you will need 'evidence' of pupils' progress, e.g. at parents' evenings, to reinforce your professional judgement.

A → **Accountability** – of you, as a professional educator. Imagine how you would feel if your doctor kept no records of your health, or the gas board did not know from one quarter to the next how much you had paid.

NB: MARRA was used until 2002 in the terminology used in the Standards for Qualified Teacher Status; we feel it is still useful to provide the full definition of the elements of MARRA.

Teachers' and pupils' views of assessment

We recently asked a number of MFL teachers and trainees to complete the sentence 'Assessment is …'. Some of their views are also used elsewhere in this book to illustrate various issues. Assessment clearly means many different things to different people, as can be seen from the selection reproduced here:

Assessment is …

- *a method for keeping up to date with the progress pupils are making, how targets are being reached and is useful for setting new targets and aiding planning. (Trainee teacher)*
- *an integral part of teaching to be used positively to inform pupils of progress, to inform further planning and target setting and as a tool for motivation. (Trainee teacher)*
- *very important for getting a good overall picture of how you and the pupils are performing and for informing future planning. (Trainee teacher)*
- *necessary to plan and give children some targets to meet; difficult because subjective sometimes; interesting (to see the children's work, what they've achieved and what you've managed to teach them!). (Experienced teacher)*
- *difficult, takes lots of time. (Experienced teacher)*
- *difficult. Lengthy to do because of four skills. Hard to carry out effectively. (Experienced teacher)*
- *formal/informal monitoring and evaluating of students' work. (Experienced teacher)*
- *important in order to monitor students' progress. (Experienced teacher)*

This list reflects the range of purposes and types of assessment, as well as the variety of personal views about assessment.

We also asked a large number of pupils from Years 7–11 in three different schools a similar question, this time with three sentence completions:

■ I think tests in Modern Foreign Languages are …
■ My homework in Modern Foreign Languages is …
■ My Modern Foreign Languages teacher helps me learn best when …

Many of the resultant statements will be used throughout the chapters in this book as appropriate. For now, here are some contributions for the first sentence from just one group of Year 7 pupils:

I think tests in Modern Foreign Languages are …

- *very easy. (Boy)*
- *hard and annoying. (Boy)*
- *a way to help you. (Boy)*
- *useful for teachers and pupils. (Girl)*
- *to see how much we have learnt in the lessons. And to move sets. (Girl)*
- *useful for teachers to understand how we are getting on in lessons. (Girl)*
- *a way to check if you understand. (Girl)*
- *to arrange pupils and assess them. (Girl)*
- *writing. (Boy)*

The pupils have covered most of the **functions** of assessment in their statements, namely:

- assessment **of** learning to allocate pupils to groups/award an achievement grade (summative assessment);
- assessment **for** learning to move learning on (formative assessment);
- assessment to inform future planning (for teachers **and** pupils) (diagnostic/formative assessment).

These pupils have also illustrated, of course, the differing reactions to being assessed. From a learner's perspective assessment can seem very daunting. If the perspective changes slightly, to encourage a feeling of acknowledged progress, to inform about what needs to be done to improve and involve learners in their own assessment, assessment will be less intimidating and more effective (see Chapter 4).

Who is assessment for?

The ultimate user of assessment information that is elicited in order to improve learning is the pupil. (Black and Wiliam 1998)

There are, of course, a number of **audiences** for assessment. The following list indicates the range of these audiences:

- individual pupil;
- groups of pupils;
- parents;
- individual teachers;
- departments;
- schools;
- LEAs;
- further and higher education institutions;
- employers;
- Government.

The audience for the assessment will influence the type of assessment undertaken; the information needed varies according to who will use it and how. Examples follow:

A A pupil needs specific feedback on his or her progress and how to improve:

> 'Remember capital letters! You have included a perfect tense – well done!'

B A parent requires information on their child's progress:

> '(Your child) has produced some very impressive pieces of writing in French and enjoys reading activities. (Your child) finds speaking more difficult and is working on his/her pronunciation. (Your child's) target is to contribute orally in class at least once every lesson.

C An individual teacher requires feedback on the appropriateness of the work and the areas where pupils need further consolidation or challenge:

> 'The end-of-unit test indicated that the majority of pupils can use the preterite endings but their use of the present tense is now confused.'

D An NQT requires evidence of his or her progress as a teacher:

▶ 'At the parents' evening I used the marks I had collected to illustrate each child's progress and to point towards their minimum targets based on the school's assessment data.'

E A department requires comparative information:

▶ 'Two parallel groups taught by different teachers in French achieved vastly different results in the assessment tests. One class performed at a much lower level in speaking than the second class.'

Reflection Task

> **Using assessment information**
>
> In each of the cases A–E above, how could you **use** the assessment information? Some suggestions are given below:
>
> - the pupil checks for capital letters;
> - the parent reminds their child of his or her personal targets and perhaps helps them (something they would certainly find more difficult with 'raw scores' or grades);
> - the teacher revisits the present tense and praises the pupils on their success with the preterite (the classic planning – teaching – assessment cycle);
> - the Head of Department carries out a mini-audit on speaking activities across the department.

In these cases and in other examples throughout this book, the link between successful assessment and more effective teaching and learning is explicit. The assessment information has been **used**.

The role of assessment in effective teaching and learning

Assessment is, naturally, a vital component in the planning – teaching – assessment cycle (see Chapter 2).

When research was carried out into effective teaching (DfEE 2000), two of the essential characteristics were given as **high expectations** and **using a range of assessment methods**. The two are, of course, linked and the learners need to be informed about both. The same report connected pupil motivation and good classroom 'climate' as arising from **effective teacher assessment and feedback**. If pupils know what they are doing, what's expected and how they can improve, they are more likely to be motivated and make progress.

A range of assessment methods includes oral and written comments and suggestions, informal and more formal 'tests', homework, quick quizzes, pupil self-evaluation. All these activities enable the teacher and the learner to look at what has been learned, what needs to be done; but this only happens if the assessment 'results' (in whatever guise) are understandable and acted upon. Blum (1984: 3–6) provides twelve characteristics of effective teaching:

1. *instruction is guided by a pre-planned curriculum;*
2. *there are high expectations for student learning;*
3. *students are carefully oriented to lessons;*
4. *instruction is clear and focused;*
5. *learning progress is monitored closely;*

> **6** *when students do not understand, they are retaught;*
> **7** *class time is used for learning;*
> **8** *there are smooth and efficient classroom routines;*
> **9** *instructional groups formed in the classroom fit instructional needs;*
> **10** *standards for classroom behaviour are high;*
> **11** *personal interactions between teachers and students are positive;*
> **12** *incentives and rewards for students are used to promote excellence.*

Effective assessment for learning contributes to the majority of these characteristics. Assessment is what makes real teaching turn into real learning rather than remaining a solo performance.

How can pupils understand the purpose of activities?

Central to effective assessment is that pupils understand why they are doing something as well as how they can improve next time. A homework task is more successful if pupils see the purpose and can make the links between it and what they have been learning in class. Similarly, one individual question used in a whole-class context may appear pointless to pupils, but if the purpose or the benchmark is clear, it attains significance. Indeed, ensuring that pupils are aware of why they are doing something and where they are aiming is an indicator of effective teaching. An example of this follows.

The class has done a simple wordsearch as a starter activity: finding a list of French words. The teacher then shows the completed wordsearch on the OHP and asks a general question: *'Vous avez trouvé quels mots?'*

Nobody answers: they see no point in supplying information which is already there.

There would be **reason** to answer:

a) if the teacher had given the words in English to find in French and the pupils therefore had to show they knew/had found the French equivalents;
b) if the teacher had emphasised that the fact that they had **found** the words was excellent, but what he or she needed now was to hear the **most accurate pronunciation** possible;
c) if there was an extra word hidden and not listed to find as a challenge.

Whatever level pupils are working at, there needs to be a sense of **purpose.** Benchmarking, expectations, objectives are all part of this – learners know where they are going and can therefore assess **themselves** properly.

> *When anyone is trying to learn, feedback about the effort has three elements: recognition of the **desired goal**, evidence about **present position** and some understanding of a **way to close the gap** between the two.* (Black and Wiliam 1998: 57)

It is very important to get the pupils articulating what they are learning and what they have understood, and give them a chance to clarify details and criteria. Although some of the suggestions below may appear quite ambitious for pupils, if you have prepared them by whole-class discussion and some pointers, these tasks can be extremely effective in helping pupils reflect on their own learning and consequently make the necessary improvements. It could be appropriate for example to ask for an explanation in English as a homework task as follows:

- What do you need to do to improve your written target language?

Or

- List the ways you are going to revise for your assessment in December.

Or

- Describe what you need to remember when you are doing your presentation in the target language. Put these into categories, e.g. language, presentation skills, resources.

These types of task are, for example, similar to those undertaken in science when detailing experiments, or in Design and Technology when indicating **how** a design brief will be fulfilled. Languages as a development of **skills** as well as knowledge should not be overlooked. Assessment includes of course preparing pupils for formal tests – i.e. how to conduct themselves in an examination or test, how things will be done, what **exactly** they have to do, etc. Any instructions have to be very clear. If the pupils are bright, they will be very frustrated if they cannot complete the task perfectly, and if less able, they will feel they are failing, and probably lose motivation.

My Modern Foreign Languages teacher helps me learn best when she explains work, because sometimes we don't understand. (Girl, 14)

Assessment is not only concerned with academic output, whether in listening, reading, speaking or writing. Successful feedback concentrates on those areas which will help learners identify issues and improve their understanding and performance. This includes developing learning strategies, attitudes, self-esteem and making connections. There are some very helpful publications on helping learners develop study and examination skills, for example Harris (1997) and Carter (2003).

Formative and summative assessment: definitions and distinctions

Essentially, the type of assessment used is really related to the **purposes** of the assessment. For example:

- To give succinct information to an audience (e.g. parents, higher education admissions tutors, pupils themselves, etc), **summative** assessment and the results thereof may be most appropriate.
- To enable a pupil to improve his or her retention of a list of vocabulary, **formative** assessment and **targeted feedback** is necessary – handing over a mark out of ten as a summative result will be most unlikely to improve his or her learning. A summative 'mark' is, in effect, a snapshot of where a pupil's knowledge and understanding have reached at a particular moment in time.

Of course, a summative assessment can also be used **formatively**, e.g. when a 'test' is discussed with pupils, possible responses brainstormed, details analysed, common errors identified and targets set.

It certainly is not the case that the distinction between formative and summative assessment depends on whether the 'test' is formal or informal. Many so-called 'informal' assessments are to all intents and purposes summative: **i.e. they result in no feedback to the pupils or reflection on the part of the pupils**. In such an instance, the reason for conducting the test at all could be questioned.

It is the usefulness of the assessment which should be paramount. If used to help learners learn and move on in their understanding, we would argue all types of assessment are valid.

All teachers assess formatively and summatively – but the formative assessment is frequently less often acknowledged and the latter often carries far more external significance, e.g. reports, parents' evenings, GCSEs. But all these outcomes are enhanced where effective formative assessment has taken and continues to take place.

Language teachers might argue that this form of assessment is even more crucial in learning a foreign language, as a skills-based subject, than in a subject where content is more to the fore. Foreign language learners need to learn how to use and structure language rather than isolated lists of individual words. For example, after learning vocabulary items successfully the learner should then progress to using them productively and manipulating them as necessary. Collecting long lists of memorised vocabulary is insufficient: examples and feedback are required to ensure the learner develops the necessary skills and knowledge to generate language.

Richard Stiggins provides the following ideas for how teachers **advance learning** rather than just check on pupils' learning:

> *They do this by:*
> - *understanding and articulating **in advance of teaching** the achievement targets that their students are to hit;*
> - *informing their students about those learning goals, **in terms that students understand,** from the very beginning of the teaching and learning process;*
> - *using classroom assessments to **build students' confidence** in themselves as learners and help them take responsibility for their own learning;*
> - *translating classroom assessment results into frequent **descriptive feedback** (versus judgmental feedback) for students, providing them with specific insights as to how to improve;*
> - *engaging students in **regular self-assessment,** with standards held constant so that students can watch themselves grow over time and thus feel in charge of their own success;*
> - *actively involving students in **communicating** with their teacher and their families about their achievement status and improvement.*
>
> *In short, the effect of assessment for learning, as it plays out in the classroom, is that students keep learning and remain confident that they can continue to learn at productive levels if they keep trying to learn. In other words, students don't give up in frustration or hopelessness.*
>
> (Stiggins 2002: 760)

Such assessment opportunities can be built into the teaching and learning process in a variety of ways. It is becoming increasingly frequent that pupils answer the register with a target language word, phrase or sentence rather than just stating their presence. This can be made more challenging by simply requiring each pupil to attempt to choose an item of language no-one else has chosen. The teacher could have chosen a 'magic' word in advance and the challenge to the pupils when answering the register is to identify it. The task can also be more targeted and differentiated by putting a class name list on an OHT, and preparing an overlay where each pupil sees exactly what they are expected to provide by way of register answer, ranging from single items to more complex phrases or idioms. Assessment opportunities do not need to be formal tests or end-of-unit assessments: they are part and parcel of the whole learning experience. It is what is done with them that is crucial.

Formative assessment: feeding back to pupils

OFSTED has commented recently on the lack of consistent formative assessment in a number of departments:

> *Assessment in Key Stage 3 often lacks rigour and, in a sample of schools, the reported levels based on teacher assessment at the end of Key Stage 3 were judged to be over-generous in nearly one school in ten. A common weakness is an over-dependence on end-of-unit tasks and summative examinations, failing to draw on the level descriptions diagnostically and formatively to assess and improve pupils' oral and written work continuously over the key stage. Routine marking in both key stages is usually regular but needs to improve in consistency and effectiveness: in a sample of schools there were shortcomings in marking in about one school in eight.* (OFSTED 2002b)

Feedback is the focus of Chapter 4. At this point, we will outline the main benefits and findings about formative assessment and feedback.

> *While formative assessment can help all pupils, it yields particularly good results with low achievers by concentrating on specific problems with their work and giving them a clear understanding of what is wrong and how to put it right.* (Black and Wiliam 1998)

 *My Modern Foreign Languages teacher helps me best when he explains things to make me understand.* (Boy, 13)

Some teachers we have spoken to are yet to be convinced that the time invested in feedback is productive, particularly for lower achievers. They also say on occasion that it can be demotivating for pupils to get feedback when their achievements are low. What is certain is that it is far more time consuming and stressful dealing with demotivated learners who have no idea where they are going and who can see no chance of improvement. This type of feedback definitely involves being honest with learners about what they need to do to improve, but does not mean every piece of work has to be labelled with a particular mark or grade. There is little to be gained by praising a piece of work or a performance to make a pupil feel better if no advice is given on what to do next. OFSTED has also commented on this:

> *Marking is usually conscientious but often fails to offer guidance on how work can be improved. In a significant minority of cases, marking reinforces underachievement and underexpectation by being too generous or unfocused.* (OFSTED 1996: 40)

Learners of all ability deserve constructive feedback on what to do to improve, albeit very small steps in some cases. Lower achieving pupils will not benefit from platitudes about good effort or destructive raw scores which show no sign of ever improving, particularly if a feeling of failure is compounded by comparison with other pupils. They need specific feedback on their own performance.

Of course, some functions of assessment can now be carried out using ICT very efficiently (see Chapters 3 and 6), and certain software can offer very specific feedback to learners (e.g. on accuracy, etc) but, ultimately, formative feedback is in the hands of the teacher and the pupil.

Assessment: more than allocating marks

It is clear that effective assessment is involved in the whole process of teaching and learning. A 'mark' can mean everything to a pupil when given huge significance by teachers, parents or peers, but may mean virtually nothing in learning terms.

Black and Wiliam (1998) point out that even where 'marks' exist in the form of records from a previous school or class, these are often not used productively by the current teacher. Records are kept and marks written down for no apparent reason. When pupils receive a mark for a piece of work or a test, any comments are often skimmed over or ignored completely. If no mark is there, the comments and advice gain in significance.

As well as getting marks back, pupils need to know how and why marks were allocated (in whatever form those marks are – whether they are levels, grades, numbers, etc). This ranges from knowing clearly that marks are awarded in a vocabulary test for correct spellings, accents, etc, to understanding what exactly 'range of expression' means and how this can be developed (see Chapter 5).

It is also important that pupils can see their progress: perhaps through the use of charts and graphs. An example of a visual representation of pupils' progress is on p117.

 2

Reflection Task

Summative or formative?

- Think of a particular class you teach or have observed. When do you think summative assessment is appropriate and when is it more appropriate to use formative assessment?

- How have you used either formative or summative assessment with that group?

Key points

- Assessment is crucial in the teaching and learning of MFL.
- It is the purpose of the assessment which determines whether it is formative or summative.
- Assessment for learning incorporates specific feedback and targets.
- Pupils benefit considerably from knowing what is expected of them.
- Effective assessment can improve pupils' achievements.

2 | Developing effective assessment practices

Chapter 1 has outlined the importance of assessment and why, what and how we assess. Assessment is a vital element in the planning process and this chapter stresses the importance of linking planning and assessment, not only using assessment information in planning but also planning for assessment opportunities. For some time Modern Foreign Languages teaching has been criticised for failing to achieve progression, especially between the key stages. With the current emphasis on raising standards, both through league tables at GCSE and the National Strategy at Key Stage 3, it is even more important to maintain records of pupils' learning and progress, and find ways of promoting learning and challenging pupils to improve their language. In this way, assessment can support progression. This chapter ends by examining indicators of good assessment practice and how all teachers, no matter what their experience, can improve assessment procedures to challenge all pupils and improve their achievement.

Linking planning and assessment

Assessment: part of the planning, teaching and learning cycle

Assessment is not a separate activity conducted at the end of a unit or at the end of the year, although clearly some elements of assessment occur in this way. It is not an end in itself, but is integral to the ongoing cycle of planning, teaching and learning.

Every contribution in a lesson, every learning task or activity, every homework or course assignment, every lesson is assessed or evaluated in some way (see the diagram on p19). Both during lessons and at the end of lessons teachers evaluate pupils' learning. Through this more informal assessment, teachers often make intuitive judgements about the effects of their teaching and identify whether learners have grasped the new vocabulary, pronunciation, structures or grammar points to determine to what extent further practice/consolidation is required, and how ready the pupils are to move on and what feedback they require. Both formal and informal assessments evaluate and assess the learning outcomes, and assessment information is used to feed back into the planning to be adjusted where necessary. (Two suggested templates for lesson planning and lesson evaluation are given on pp22–24 and can also be found on the associated website – see Web templates 1 and 2).

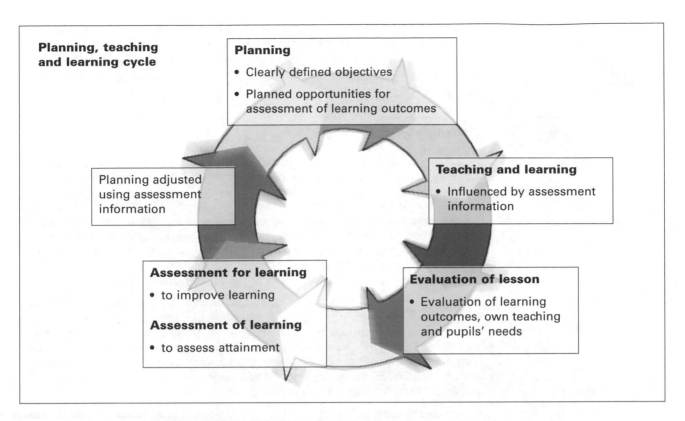

Planning, teaching and learning cycle

Planning
- Clearly defined objectives
- Planned opportunities for assessment of learning outcomes

Teaching and learning
- Influenced by assessment information

Planning adjusted using assessment information

Evaluation of lesson
- Evaluation of learning outcomes, own teaching and pupils' needs

Assessment for learning
- to improve learning

Assessment of learning
- to assess attainment

Planning for learning

A lesson plan is part of the overall planning for learning. The diagram below illustrates how lesson plans are the realisation of schemes of work and overall frameworks. Overarching all planning is the need to achieve pupils' progress.

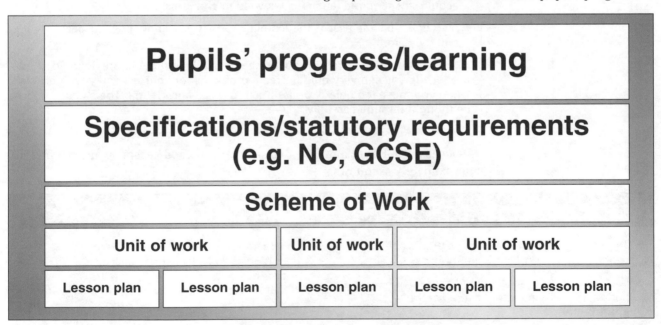

Pupils' progress/learning

Specifications/statutory requirements (e.g. NC, GCSE)

Scheme of Work

Unit of work		Unit of work		Unit of work
Lesson plan	Lesson plan	Lesson plan	Lesson plan	Lesson plan

This overall goal of pupils' progress relates to **long-term planning**. Schemes of work are built around National Curriculum requirements, examination specifications and other frameworks (perhaps specific to the school context). **Medium-term plans** are then created from the Scheme of Work to cover, for example, a half term's work with smaller units of work and lesson plans. Clearly, then, lesson plans are not 'one-off' plans, but a constituent part of pupils' learning, and part of that continuum.

To plan effectively, the teacher needs to look **backwards** to what pupils already know and have done, and **forwards** to what they will do next and in the longer term. Lesson plans stemming from effective and comprehensive long- and medium-term planning are inevitably more coherent and give more opportunities for progression.

Trainee/NQT Task

Thinking about planning

As a trainee teacher it is not only essential to plan lessons and series of lessons carefully, but also to record this planning, i.e. to have a hard copy of your thought processes and evaluations. You need to provide evidence of your effective planning (see for example the QtT Standards, TTA 2002), and it is also necessary to prove to the teachers whose classes you are taking that the pupils will continue to progress. These teachers remain responsible for the pupils' learning throughout your time in the school. As you progress in your career, carefully recorded evidence of your planning and pupils' achievements will stand you in good stead for your own professional development.

When teaching your own native language or a foreign language you have studied to a high level, your competence in that language is clearly good. As a teacher, you need to use that knowledge and transform the language into something which is 'teachable' by you and therefore 'learnable' by your learners: bombarding them with unstructured torrents of language will clearly not be effective, similarly, limiting the language input to a very restricted diet will not help their progress. You must:

- plan what exactly you wish your learners to be able to do (learning objectives: linguistic, communicative, cultural);

- plan how you will enable them to do this (for example, the manageable steps you will guide them through to achieve their aim);

- plan which resources you will exploit and produce to help your learners acquire the required language knowledge and skills;

- plan how you will assess the learning so that you know how successful you and they are.

If you don't think carefully about the exact language to be learned (and produced), you can very quickly create problems for yourself and your learners when you move too quickly or assume too much knowledge. The steps need to be thought through carefully.

A successful MFL lesson (the realisation of a good lesson plan) might look approximately as follows.

LESSON PLAN

- Target language atmosphere as pupils come in to room (Music? Display? Smell? Words? Objects?)

- Warm-up/starter (not token gesture but pedagogically valuable) plus register (if appropriate)

- Objectives (clear and useful, oral and written)

- Activities in lesson which 'get pupils learning':
  - correctly sequenced (in its simplest form: presentation/practice/production);
  - differentiated (matched);
  - focus on whole class/individual/pair/group as appropriate;

- consideration to learner perspective;
- transitions and instructions: clear and appropriate;
- activities available for pupils who finish work set

- Assessment/evaluation built in

- Summaries/target setting/homework

But however impressive the atmosphere, the resources or the activities, without **assessment** the lesson remains a 'one-off'. Lesson planning could be seen as a process of decision making – which is then another process of decision making in the classroom and afterwards. Evaluations and assessment are a major contribution to the planning and decision-making process. The focus of any lesson and any sequence of lessons should be the learner and their learning. The learner should always be at the centre.

Stating the lesson objectives at the start of a lesson is a clear way of informing pupils what they are going to learn and what activities they are going to be involved in. Written objectives on the (interactive) whiteboard or OHP can form the framework to a lesson and key transitions can be indicated as pupils can see clearly the shape and progress of the lesson as items are ticked off. A final summing up and re-cap of what has been learned at the end of the lesson from the teacher and the pupils gives pupils a sense of achievement. Objectives made explicit to pupils act as a basis for assessment, self-evaluation and target setting.

Planning lessons

Planning and careful preparation, then, are fundamental to good teaching and learning. The lesson plan, outline and evaluation templates on pp22–24 are designed to be used by trainees primarily (see also website, Web templates 1 and 2). The lesson plan template includes details of learning objectives, differentiation strategies, assessment opportunities, homework, resources needed and the lesson outline which should also, with current legislation, note NC Attainment Target and Level. In addition we include a useful checklist to ensure there is a balance of skills, balance of interaction (whole, group, pair, individual), a variety of learning styles and cross-curricular opportunities over time. All teachers will benefit from the thinking process involved, even though their plans will not usually contain so much detail.

Heads of Department, subject mentors and members of the departmental team can all help to monitor the work of a trainee in the department and some of the ideas for evaluating lessons could be used by all teachers. By using the template here carefully, trainees will be more likely to have successful, interesting lessons, to evaluate pupils' learning more effectively and keep more accurate records of pupils' (and their own) progress. The template can be tailored to suit individuals, can be adapted as the trainee progresses, and as it is available electronically via the associated website, it can be personalised (e.g. amount of space, order of elements, etc).

Lesson plan format: MFL PGCE
University of Warwick

Previous targets set by mentors/tutors relevant to this lesson:

Essential Information					
Language:	Class:	Day:	Date:	Period/time:	Room:
No. of pupils:	Level of ability:		No. with IEPs/statements:		

Learning Objectives	
Communicative:	Linguistic: Core: Peripheral:
Cultural:	Skills:

Differentiation Strategies/Providing CHALLENGE					
Core:		Extension:		Consolidation:	
Balance of Skills:		AT1	AT2	AT3	AT4
Balance of Interaction:		Whole Class	Pair Work	Individual	Group
Learning Styles:		Visual		Auditory	Kinaesthetic
Previous Learning Outcomes					
Expected Learning Outcomes					

Assessment Opportunities	
During lesson	After lesson

Cross-curricular Opportunities						
Moral	Social	Cultural	Spiritual	Literacy	Numeracy	ICT

Materials/Resources (in addition to 'classroom kit')					
Cassette/ recorder	CDROM/ software	Video player/ camera	Flash cards/ visuals/ OHTs	Worksheets	Cue cards
Opportunities for using ICT					

Homework		
Task:	Assessment criteria:	Due date:
Notes/notices		
Alternative/contingency		

Lesson outline

Learning Objectives	
Communicative:	Linguistic: Core: Peripheral:
Cultural:	Skills:

NB: Number of activities is, of course, variable!

TIME	Activities	NC (AT, PoS, Level) (or appropriate curricular info.)
	Warm-up/introduction/register (plus opportunities for feedback) Shared objectives (what you will say, what you will write): (e.g. by the end of the lesson you will be able to …) Main body of lesson: (including TL instructions, transitions, signposting) Activity 1: (including TL instructions, example, demonstration) Activity 2: (including TL instructions, example, demonstration) Activity 3: (including TL instructions, example, demonstration) Activity 4: (including TL instructions, example, demonstration) Homework setting: (what you will say, what you will write) Summary/finishing off/target setting:	

Developing effective assessment practices

Ask yourself:	Yes	No	Pupils
If I were a lazy pupil in your class, could I have got away with doing very little?			
If I were a very able pupil in your class, would I have felt challenged?			
If I were a lower ability pupil in your class, would I have felt lost or confused?			
If I were a shy pupil in your class, would I nevertheless have had chance to contribute orally in some way?			
If I were a hard-working pupil in your class, would I have felt praised and my achievement acknowledged?			
Would a pupil in your class be able to summarise what they had learnt during the lesson?			
Would a pupil in your class be able to describe how they could improve their learning?			
Your comments on:			
Lesson start			
Lesson end			
Instructions			
Transitions			
Activities			
Use of TL			
Matching/differentiation			
Assessment - how?			
Involvement of all pupils?			
Timing			
Resources			
Your explanations of any questions/misconceptions			
Pace			
Pupils' learning			
Pupils' behaviour			
Pupils' understanding of 'what they were supposed to do'			
Pupils' interest and involvement			
Comments on listening			
Comments on speaking			
Comments on reading			
Comments on writing			
What linguistic difficulties do you think the pupils experienced?			
Targets/action points for future lessons:			

Planning assessment opportunities in lessons and sequences of lessons

In order to plan assessment opportunities effectively a range of decisions need to be made:

- **why** the assessment is being carried out (measuring learning outcomes against objectives, diagnosing strengths and weaknesses, forward planning);
- **what** exactly is being assessed (vocabulary items, grammatical structures, communicative competence, cultural content);
- **at what point** assessment should take place;
- **how** the assessment will be conducted (individually/in pairs/whole class, discrete skill or multi-skill, informally by observation or formally);
- **by whom** the assessment will be conducted (by teacher alone, by peers, by a combination of both).

During the course of planning, (either short, medium or long term), assessment opportunities should be clearly mapped. Informal assessment may build up overall judgements about how well a class is performing, including being aware that a particular pupil is not coping too well and that another seems to have made more rapid progress. However, this more informal feedback needs to be supplemented by a specific assessment of every individual. Teachers need to know to what extent each member of the group has met the learning objectives, so that they can offer the right help or guidance at a personal level, to feed back and therefore help learning to progress (assessment **for** learning) and to build up a record of marks in each Attainment Target over a period of time (assessment **of** learning). Therefore, you need to think about which activities could and should be assessed in each lesson (formatively/summatively); how you will assess them (particularly with regard to assessing speaking as an ongoing process); how you can give instant feedback and targets by marking some work in class.

Assessment activities should be planned into the schedule of learning, be chosen very carefully, and have a specific focus or purpose which is clear to the learner. They should include a variety of task types designed to fit smoothly into the lesson and should allow learners a clear sense of satisfaction. Pupils need to be able to show their attainment at an appropriate range of levels across all four Attainment Targets, although not necessarily in each lesson. (Ideas for assessing each of the Attainment Targets are included in Chapter 5.)

Formative assessment with feedback and targets to help improve progress should be a routine part of learning and should use the kinds of tasks with which pupils are already familiar. It is important to choose tasks which will assess appropriate learning goals, while enabling pupils to perform at their highest level of ability. A task to help trainees develop the planning, delivery, marking and recording of assessment is contained in Chapter 7.

 2

Trainee/NQT Task

> **Departmental information**
>
> Early in your school placement/in your induction year make sure you obtain and discuss the department's curriculum/syllabus documents and schemes of work for the classes to be observed and/or taught, including policies and procedures for assessment.

Progression and assessment

For some time OFSTED reports have included comments on the difficulties encountered in achieving progression in MFL from year to year and across the key stages and have highlighted **progression** as one of the main factors requiring attention in MFL teaching. The longevity of this issue is indicated in the following quotes:

> *Within Key Stage 3, standards of achievement are better in Years 7 and 8 than in Year 9.* (OFSTED 1995)

> *Pupils make a good start in Year 7 but make less progress over the five years of compulsory secondary education than in most other subjects.* (OFSTED 1999)

The OFSTED report 1999/2000 raised improving progress and continuity 11–18 as an issue some schools should continue to address and the most recent report, while recognising that 'the gradual improvement in the quality of teaching of recent years continues', nevertheless emphasised that:

> *More attention to progression and to raising expectations of pupils' use of the foreign language is needed in planning.* (OFSTED 2002b)

Why is progression an issue?

Many teachers consider that learning languages through topics in some instances restricted development in language competence and led to recycling topics from KS3 to KS4 without extending linguistic structures or any clear sense of progression. The nature of topics has often proved demotivating and has led to rote learning of set phrases rather than real linguistic understanding and competence.

What can help improve progression?

Schemes of work need to include detailed plans for progression, so that substantial repetition of the same material does not occur from year to year and key stage to key stage, and that if topics are revisited then these are revised, built on and extended linguistically and cognitively. Progression in language learning can be achieved by recycling language across topics, introducing non topic-specific language and showing pupils how to manipulate language in different situations as well as helping pupils to develop learning skills. The National Curriculum 2000 heralded a move away from the topic approach to greater emphasis on the understanding and application of grammar in order to achieve greater progression. By auditing coverage of the PoS (see p30), departments can achieve greater progression in these areas. This provides an exciting opportunity to evaluate MFL teaching and learning and look afresh at what is happening in the classroom in order to improve both the learning experience and attainment.

Planning for progression

Planning for progression is not always straightforward; progression in language learning involves a complex range of elements. It refers to a broadening of contexts in content; a development of each of the four skills of listening, speaking, reading and writing, as well as language-learning skills; a deepening acquisition of linguistic knowledge and ability; and an expansion of cultural awareness. The National Curriculum Council non-statutory guidance for England and Wales (1992: D2) suggested progression should be built into MFL planning in a number of ways: from concrete ideas to abstract, from simple aspects to complex, from specific themes to general, from factual topics to non-factual, from classroom experiences to the wider world, from familiar contexts to unfamiliar and from less controversial aspects to more controversial. This demonstrates that progression is far from linear and requires considerable thought and planning to ensure progression is built into lesson plans, medium-term plans and schemes of work.

 3

Trainee/NQT Task

How do we manifest progression in MFL learning?

- Write down a list of opportunities to encourage pupil progression in each Attainment Target.
- How would each opportunity match with the National Curriculum level descriptions?
- What levels could pupils reach?

In order to achieve progression we could:

- raise learners' expectations of what they can achieve and encourage the ability to cope with more demanding tasks;
- develop pupils' knowledge and use of vocabulary and sentence structure to include a range and variety of language;
- develop pupils' ability to initiate and sustain TL use;
- allow fluency without correction but hold a place for intensive grammar teaching and ensure learners are aware of the difference;
- link new items with more familiar language and help pupils make corrections;
- transfer knowledge across topic areas, helping pupils build language frameworks which are independent of topic;
- teach pupils to take in more language from memory and help them with learning strategies;
- provide opportunities for pupils to use language creatively, contributing their own ideas and adapting language;
- promote more autonomous learning;
- use level descriptions and target setting productively and constructively – not for their own sake;
- introduce a wide lexis and build pupils' self-esteem through this;
- challenge pupils (linguistically and intellectually).

It is vital to be totally familiar with the assessment criteria relevant to the age and classes taught. Knowing the final destination, that is, the type of work required in order to achieve a certain level or grade, is helpful both for teachers and pupils (see further details in Chapter 5). Many teachers when following a course book, fall into the trap of assuming it provides all that is necessary. Planning for progression entails looking critically at the course book and materials available, judging the levels targeted and in many cases extending the material in order to challenge pupils to reach their potential. Teachers are responsible for making sure pupils know what they are aiming at and planning opportunities for them to achieve this. Current legislation provides NC level descriptions in each Attainment Target and it is important for teachers to consider carefully at which level pupils have the opportunity to work in each lesson. Level descriptions help to determine the level of challenge and to plan for progression. Trainees are often concerned that they are working at very low levels with their pupils. It is natural that when presenting new items of language at the start of a unit/topic/module, pupils may be working at levels 1 and 2. What is important is to think of ways of making the work progress to higher levels as rapidly as possible by linking the new items with known structures/different tenses or introducing more advanced structures in order to provide sufficient challenge. Encouraging pupils to be aware of what is expected at different levels and how they can improve their work can help them to achieve a higher level. Many schools display pupil-friendly level descriptions (see Chapter 5) to make the assessment criteria transparent and to focus on what needs to be done to progress. Self evaluation and setting targets are crucial elements in this process (see Chapter 4).

Trainee/NQT Task

Linguistic progression

Your pupils (Year 9) have just learned vocabulary for jobs and professions.

• What will you do next to ensure linguistic progression?

• Make a note of the next stages in learning and further activities to exploit this new knowledge.

Evaluating lessons

Assessment of pupils' learning takes place throughout the lesson and, in a more reflective way, afterwards. If a lesson 'goes well', it's important to establish why (and vice versa). This evaluation should inform future planning and provide evidence for pupils' progress. It is important to comment on pupils' learning of individual teaching points, not just their behaviour or a general impression. The evaluation structure outlined below is designed to help make this analysis rigorous, yet straightforward.

Evaluation structure

The following points could be used in discussion with a subject mentor/tutor in conjunction with lesson observation feedback.

- Good **and** bad factors – address all aspects
- How involved were the pupils? Did I just show off?
- Were there any 'incidents' (time wasting/distractions/latecomers) – how did I handle them?
- What would I do differently next time?
- Did I plan enough/too much?
- Did I use TL predominantly? And appropriately?
- Any equipment/resources/organisational problems?
- What did the pupils learn and how am I going to check?
- How was my use of TL during the lesson? And that of the pupils?
- Did the lesson build successfully on work that had preceded it, i.e. was there successful progression?
- Was the lesson timed well or were sections rushed or extended unnecessarily?
- How did I incorporate the four AT's (as appropriate) and the PoS?
- Did I ensure maximum participation from **all** pupils?

- How well did I use resources/materials? How appropriate were the resources chosen? Were there problems or inaccuracies I should have spotted in advance?
- How did my differentiation strategies work? Did they support/stretch the learners sufficiently?
- Did the pupils learn what I wanted them to?
- How would I evaluate the progress of individual pupils/groups of pupils? (Don't be tempted to assess progress in terms of 'the class' – there is more to it than this!)

For further evaluation questions see the lesson evaluation template on p24 or visit the website (see Web template 2). These questions have been developed in response to trainee, mentor and tutor reactions and comments. They include a series of questions relating directly to pupils' learning and experiences, and trainees have commented that the questions have been very successful in helping them analyse the effectiveness of their teaching, investigate pupils' learning and plan subsequent learning based on the evaluation questions.

Self-evaluation of lessons is the first stage in professional development. Being observed and receiving constructive feedback, and setting future targets and acting on them assist further development. As teaching experience develops and evaluating lessons comes more easily, it becomes possible to evaluate a **series** of lessons, i.e. how well the learning objectives were met over a **unit** of work and what needs to be done next.

**Head of
Department
Task**

Peer observation

Much can be learned by observing colleagues and being observed. Provided peer observation is non-threatening and seeks to feed back constructively and objectively, it can prove to be a positive way of monitoring planning, teaching and learning, and assessment. This can help to raise standards by setting priorities for improvement.

- Create a series of planned observations within the department and ensure feedback is provided.

Assessing coverage of the National Curriculum

More teachers need to take into account the full range of the Programme of Study in their planning, and to use assessment more effectively. (OFSTED 2002b)

While planning for Key Stages 3 and 4, constant reference to the NC document is crucial as this provides a clear framework of what is expected. The Programme of Study supplies a checklist of what pupils are required to be taught. We provide a template to audit your coverage of the Programme of Study on p30 (see also Web template 3). By referring to this regularly during planning it is easier to see what knowledge, language skills, language-learning skills, cultural awareness and breadth of study have been covered over a period of time. To check that current practice genuinely reflects the requirements of the NC, it is advisable to carry out an audit of what aspects are being covered adequately and what aspects might need further attention within a department.

Programme of Study – Key Stages 3 and 4

March coverage ▼

Knowledge, skills and understanding

Acquiring knowledge and understanding of the target language

1 Pupils should be taught:

a	The principles and interrelationship of sounds and writing in the target language;	✔	✔	✔	✔	
b	The grammar of the target language and how to apply it;	✔	✔	✔	✔	
c	How to express themselves using a range of vocabulary and structures	✔	✔	✔	✔	

Developing language skills

2 Pupils should be taught:

a	How to listen carefully for gist & detail;	✔	✔	✔	✔	
b	Correct pronunciation and intonation;	✔	✔	✔	✔	
c	How to ask and answer questions;	✔	✔	✔	✔	
d	How to initiate and develop conversations;				✔	
e	How to vary the target language to suit context, audience and purpose;	✔	✔	✔	✔	
f	How to adapt language they already know for different contexts;	✔	✔	✔	✔	
g	Strategies for dealing with the unpredictable;		✔			
h	Techniques for skimming and for scanning written texts for information, including those from ICT-based sources;		✔			
i	How to summarise and report the main points of spoken or written texts, using notes where appropriate;					
j	How to redraft their writing to improve its accuracy and presentation, including the use of ICT					

Developing language-learning skills

3 Pupils should be taught:

a	Techniques for memorising words, phrases and short extracts;					
b	How to use context and other clues to interpret meaning;	✔	✔	✔	✔	
c	To use their knowledge of English or another language when learning the target language;	✔	✔	✔	✔	
d	How to use dictionaries & reference materials appropriately and effectively;	✔	✔	✔	✔	
e	How to develop their independence in learning and using the target language					

Developing cultural awareness

4 Pupils should be taught about different countries and cultures by:

a	Working with authentic materials in the target language, including some from ICT-based sources;	✔	✔	✔	✔	
b	Communicating with native speakers;	✔	✔	✔	✔	
c	Considering their own culture and comparing it with the cultures of the countries and communities where the target language is spoken;					
d	Considering the experiences and perspectives of people in these countries and communities					

Breadth of Study

5 During Key Stages 3 and 4, pupils should be taught the Knowledge, skills and understanding through:

a	Communicating in the target language in pairs & groups, and with their teacher;	✔	✔	✔	✔	
b	Using everyday classroom events as an opportunity for spontaneous speech;					
c	Expressing and discussing personal feelings and opinions;					
d	Producing and responding to different types of spoken and written language, including texts produced using ICT;	✔	✔	✔	✔	
e	Using a range of resources, including ICT, for accessing and communicating information;	✔	✔	✔	✔	
f	Using the target language creatively and imaginatively;		✔	✔	✔	
g	Listening, reading or viewing for personal interest and enjoyment, as well as for information;				✔	
h	Using the target language for real purposes;	✔	✔	✔	✔	
i	Working in a variety of contexts, including everyday activities, personal and social life, the world around us, the world of work and the international world.				✔	

Reflection Task

3

> **Long-term/medium-term planning**
>
> Carry out an audit of your coverage of the Programme of Study using Web template 3.
>
> - Work through each statement of the PoS.
> - Reflect how often you teach these aspects to your KS3 pupils.
> - Consider which areas are well/poorly covered.
> - How effectively have they been learned?
> - Think about how you could use this to adjust your future planning.
>
> (By downloading the PoS grid from the associated website, items can be highlighted or columns created to form a grid and dated to show coverage over a period of time as in the example on p30.)

Indicators of good assessment practice for trainees/NQTs and more experienced teachers

Assessment is a complex process and involves a wide range of varying activities, including, for example:

- knowledge of relevant assessment criteria for each age group;
- monitoring pupils' progress in class;
- consolidation of learning through homework;
- informal and formal assessment of attainment for both formative and summative purposes;
- use of assessment data to inform lesson planning;
- informal and formal feedback to pupils with appropriate targets set;
- maintenance of accurate records;
- reporting to parents.

Deciding how effectively a teacher uses assessment in his or her teaching needs more than a gut feeling: just as when assessing pupils' linguistic performance, criteria are needed to be able to judge teachers' practice. Most teacher training institutions develop descriptors or pen portraits to help tutors and mentors make judgements in the assessment of student teachers.

Below is a description of Teacher A, who is meeting the requirements for Qualified Teacher Status. Read the description through, then choose the appropriate task from the Task boxes below.

Teacher A: characteristics of good assessment practice

- Uses a range of strategies to make accurate assessments of pupils' achievements; uses these assessments to inform planning and teaching.
- Lesson plans are cross-referenced with relevant Programme of Study (PoS), syllabuses and level descriptors, where appropriate.
- Sets suitable objectives for sequences of lessons and plans how they will be assessed.
- Provides opportunities to consolidate classroom learning and sets homework in line with school/departmental policies.
- Produces some evidence of improved teaching through self evaluation and target setting over a period of time.

- Is familiar with and understands the basic subject framework (relevant programmes of study, level and end of key stage descriptions).
- Displays accurate knowledge of section of specification being taught and some awareness of how it fits into the whole.
- Able to evaluate extent to which learning objectives have been achieved and take appropriate action, including where ICT has been used.
- Makes assessment of pupils' understanding during teaching and gives feedback to pupils; encourages pupils to reflect on their own performance.
- Provides constructive oral and written feedback on pupils' work and sets targets based on this.
- Monitors strengths and weaknesses using focused observation, questioning and testing, as appropriate; uses and assesses ICT as appropriate.
- Maintains adequate records of pupils' work and achievements in order to provide evidence of progress and attainment.
- Familiar with statutory and school policy requirements on assessment and reporting to parents.
- Accurate knowledge of relevant assessment requirements and procedures for NC, KS4 and post-16.
- Knows how national, local and school data can be used to set targets for pupils' achievement.
- Shows appropriate use of routine assessment procedures including NC and other standardised tests.

Trainee/NQT Task

Characteristics of good assessment practice

- Decide how your practice matches up with the description here.

- Work out how this satisfactory description could be improved: what factors would make this practice excellent?

- Then have a look at INSET/ITE Task 4 (p131) in Chapter 7 for descriptors of teachers' assessment practice at good and very good levels.

Head of Department Task

Characteristics of good assessment practice

- Consider how you might use the characteristics of good assessment practice set out above to help evaluate your performance and that of the department.

- Look at INSET/ITE Task 4 (p131) in Chapter 7 for the full range of pen portraits of teachers and their assessment practice and consider whether it would be useful for your department, or for creating action plans for individual teachers.

Using these indicators of current practice, a picture can be built up of what areas need to be focused on, whether individually or as a department.

Key points

- There is a wide range of activities involved in the process of effective assessment.

- All teachers can find ways of improving assessment procedures to fit coherently into planning in order to motivate and challenge pupils' learning.

- Effective assessment is a key element in achieving progression: assessing what pupils have learnt and using that information to plan the next stage in learning.

- Assessment is not simply about collecting marks with no purpose, but can impact directly on pupils' learning by providing feedback to show pupils what they know, how they can make the most of what they know, and how they can improve. Communicating this clearly to pupils is one factor in raising expectations and attainment.

- Assessment and effective feedback are an aid to progression and a fundamental constituent in the process of developing challenging work for pupils.

- Teachers and pupils need to be aware of the level at which they are performing and pupils need to be given guidelines and advice about how to improve.

3

Making assessment work – practicalities

Effective learning takes place largely as a result of skilful informal assessment, through clear articulation of standards and expectations, and through feedback and encouragement, rather than through the 'carrot and stick' of examinations, the knowledge for which is often quickly forgotten. (Stobart and Gipps 1997: 78)

This chapter suggests some ways forward to evaluate and improve your own assessment practice and that of the department. It includes some fundamental information about recording learners' progress, which is aimed primarily at trainee teachers or NQTs, but which may also be appropriate for Heads of Department or other more experienced teachers who are considering their assessment policies and practices and those of their colleagues. Of course, a great deal of information should be available to the HoD on a school level which can then be utilised for departmental, class and individual targets.

Also included in this chapter are specific examples of assessment in practice. Homework and vocabulary learning are used to illustrate some of the issues.

Basic considerations for teachers of MFL

Without assessment (in all its guises) how would we ever find out such things as:

Some of the quiet girls sitting near the back of the class, who hardly ever contribute in lessons, had exercise books which were extremely neat, methodical and conscientious, and achieved good results in class exercises, homework and listening tests. Comments written on their books also indicated surprisingly lively personalities. On the other hand, one boy who is extremely keen and volunteers constantly in class, had a very untidy book with a surprising number of mistakes, and, to some extent, over enthusiasm. (Comments from a trainee teacher after analysing the work of one class)

The 'revelations' above will be familiar to most readers of this book: it is the professional use of monitoring and assessment which informs teachers in this way; from scanning a whole class during pairwork to collating marks in a formal examination. But how is this assessment best carried out, recorded and above all used?

To help learners learn more effectively, you need to be able to answer the following questions, all of which form part of effective assessment, and have the information readily available to share with others and to inform your own planning:

1 How much and what does the learner already know/understand? What can the learner already do?
2 How does the learner learn best and how can you find out?
3 How can you assess in a way that enables learners to feel they are succeeding, but without patronising them or avoiding the real issues?
4 How can feedback be used most effectively with learners of different abilities?
5 How best can you record learners' progress?
6 What happens once a 'mark' has been awarded, i.e. what action is taken by the teacher/learner?

A combination of existing records and formative and summative assessment can provide some answers to these questions. Some suggestions are given below.

What does the learner already know and what can the learner do?

Some answers to this question will be discovered through schemes of work and available assessment records. But much of the information will be gained through working with the learners in the class and by evaluating their work and responses in lessons and from homework (see Chapters 2 and 4, as well as departmental tasks later in this chapter). Using records already available is very important: otherwise a teacher is starting to assess in a vacuum and previous records and evaluations are wasted.

How does the learner learn best and how do you find out?

There have been some excellent publications recently in this area (e.g. Graham 1997, also Harris 1997, and Grenfell and Harris 1999, Macaro 2001, Carter 2003). Learning styles and learner strategies need to form part of an approach to assessment.

To illustrate different learning styles we asked a large number of pupils from Years 7–11 to complete a sentence.

My Modern Foreign Languages teacher helps me best when ...

- *we listen to tapes.* (Boy, 11)
- *she goes through grammar on the board.* (Girl, 13)
- *she explains something and then gives lots of examples.* (Boy, 14)
- *when we do verb revision.* (Boy, 16)
- *she does oral lessons so I can experience talking it.* (Girl, 15)
- *we discuss and have sheets to help us.* (Girl, 16)

- *she explains things to me on my own. (Girl, 15)*
- *she explains things in English and French so I know and can get an understanding of the words. (Girl, 11)*
- *I do a test. (Girl 12)*
- *she goes over my mistakes. (Boy, 12)*
- *I read through what we've done. (Girl, 15)*
- *we have a fun lesson because I remember it. (Girl, 13)*
- *he plays games because you have to remember the words to play the game. (Boy, 12)*
- *we start a new module. The teacher goes over it well. (Girl, 12)*
- *she uses pictures. (Boy, 13)*
- *she gets us to repeat. (Girl, 12)*
- *I am working on my own on grammar work. (Boy, 13)*
- *we get an independent homework. (Girl, 14)*
- *I work in groups. (Boy, 14)*

The pupils' responses above relate directly to their preferred learning styles and activities, even though the original focus of the sentence was on what their **teacher** does. It has become very popular to consider and incorporate learning styles into teaching and learning programmes; indeed some of these are listed in the lesson plan template (Web template 1) on p22 (visual/auditory/kinaesthetic). These approaches have proved very successful. It is further evidence for the value of planning a variety of activities, incorporating a range of media and resources, and providing a balance of language skills. This applies to homework too, of course (see p53).

Reflection Task

Accounting for learner preferences

- Look at the pupil responses in the list above.

- How many different preferences are mentioned or implied (for example, visuals)?

- Would all the pupils have encountered their preferred activity/style at some stage in your recent lessons?

- Perhaps you could consider carrying out a similar survey with the pupils you teach: this may be particularly helpful with a class you are finding challenging or who are not achieving expected targets.

Learner styles can be accommodated by the teacher, for example by varying the way listening activities are handled. Consider the different styles appealed to in the following listening tasks. The text is a person describing his or her family. After some whole-class revision/consolidation work on the language needed (anagrams to be solved in pairs, quick-fire individual questions and answers), the listening task is introduced.

Task A

Pupils hear a description of the person's family and simultaneously see a list of target language questions on the OHP based on the text, for example: *Wie alt ist meine Mutter?*

They hear the text twice, work on their answers individually and answers are then collated by the teacher orally on a whole-class basis.

Task B Pupils hear a description of the person's family and make their own notes on the text expanding on a mind map (below) provided on the whiteboard:

43 Jahre alt

Vater   Mutter   Geschwister   Haustiere

After the second hearing, they pool ideas with their partner.

They are then shown the list of questions mentioned in Task A, and work on their answers together, before answers are collated and checked as a whole class. The text is then played again, and any clarifications given or queries answered.

Each of these tasks may be appropriate in different circumstances, but they produce and develop very different skills in the learners, using the same basic text. Task B allows for more differentiation and challenge, and avoids the 'right answer' or 'defeatist' scenarios often arising from lists of questions. In addition, task B provides good evidence of pupils' listening ability and study skills, as well as giving them a chance to show what they **do** hear rather than what they miss.

How can I assess learners so they feel they are succeeding?

Teachers are responsible for learners' progress and monitoring that progress. A mainstay of this responsibility is ensuring learners know how to improve. If learners receive empty praise or encouragement, it will achieve almost nothing – they may feel reasonably happy, but will have no idea about how to improve next time. If a learner consistently receives very low grades, the sense of failure and de-motivation is understandable. It is, however, not helpful to gloss over problems or patronise pupils with vacuous praise.

A very important question (included on the evaluation template on p24 – Web template 2) asks whether the learners would be able to describe how they could improve their learning. It is in this area that the appropriate use of comments and marks is crucial. What exactly is a 'mark'? What does it mean? What does it communicate? Who needs to know it? Recording effort as well as achievement is crucial – but how?

Every 'mark' you record should pass the following test: why am I writing this down? If the answer is 'I have no idea', then what use is the mark?

What does a 'mark' enable you to say or do, and what does it do for the learner? There is a clear link, for example, between recorded 'marks' and parents' evenings (see Chapter 6). Recorded marks to monitor progress, and comments, questions and feedback to improve learning are both crucial. But every time a mark is awarded by you for your records, it does not necessarily have to be seen by the pupil. Its purpose may be very different: for example to compare one group's performance with a previous cohort. There will be occasions where it is productive and motivating for a pupil to see a score or grade that is awarded – there are other occasions when it is not.

To enable pupils to feel they are achieving and they know their goals, benchmarks and criteria along with examples of good answers should be readily apparent. If pupils can see concretely what progress they are making and what they still need to do, they will feel more in control of their learning.

For example, for Key Stage 4 pupils, one of their self-evaluation criteria for any written or oral piece could be to ensure they are incorporating new structures and linguistic items by underlining or colour coding any language they were already familiar with at Key Stage 3 or, conversely, highlight any new structures they are using. This can be extended into pairwork and group work, where responses to a written task are selected by the teacher, sections copied (anonymously) onto a sheet of paper or onto OHT and in pairs or groups students decide how the work could be improved.

For KS3 or KS4 learners, this could be achieved by dividing the class into four or five groups, each with a basic 'text' (this may be as short as one or two sentences). Each group is given an 'improvement factor' (e.g. adjectives, tense, 'because') and has to improve their text accordingly. These are then shared and combined to produce a whole, more impressive text.

Visualisation is an accepted element in the training of top class athletes and sports people, enabling them to envisage what success feels like, what is needed and how they can achieve and improve. A similar process can be used in teaching. If models, benchmarks and goals are not presented and empty praise or bald scores given in a vacuum, learners of any ability will not progress satisfactorily. Restricting learners to a narrow achievement area is unfair. It should also be clear that making mistakes is OK and a normal part of learning (see Chapter 4)! When developing departmental schemes of work, this could include producing benchmarks and models for key pieces of work for learners to work towards and in some cases surpass. These models could be added to or replaced by real examples from learners. A departmental task might be to identify key tasks in the scheme of work which will be attempted by all pupils: moderation and comparison is much more straightforward in this instance, both across year groups and between cohorts. The models need to be at an appropriate and attainable level for the pupils, of course.

It is also useful to produce your own answers to GCSE questions, A level tasks, textbook exercises, completed in the same conditions as the pupils. What would **you** do? Could you use your answers to exemplify strategies etc? How would you tackle a particular task? What could you do to improve your response? Which bit did you tackle first? How did you prepare? This activity can reveal issues and strategies which can help learners work out their own approaches.

Creating a positive assessment climate

There is of course a lot to be said for creating a positive and constructive atmosphere in the classroom. Black et al (2002) suggest a more unusual approach to asking pupils to put their hands up when they know the answer: they offer the possibility of asking them **not** to raise their hands, with the assumption that everyone will have an answer, even if it is 'I don't know'. This is a useful approach in MFL: if pupils can legitimately answer in the target language with 'I don't know', 'I don't understand', etc, it is more productive (and informative for the teacher) than concentrating on those who **do** know. Another approach in this vein may be to ask all the class to start with their hands up, or to confer about the answer for five seconds with their partner before raising their hands. Similarly, many departments are now using small whiteboards for pupils to display answers, responses or opinions individually or in pairs. This method can be very good for assessing knowledge of vocabulary, understanding of listening, etc.

The positive atmosphere and constructive assessment needed to progress can be helped by brief whole-class feedback and targets after a piece of work. For example: you have taken in and marked a piece of homework. Pupils presented some survey information in a graph, and linguistically all of them neglected to differentiate between singular and plural in their summary sentences. The presentation of the graphs was wonderful! **Both** elements can feature in targeted feedback at the start of the lesson.

How best can I record learners' progress?

The importance of good, informative records which can be passed on is clear: the transition from primary to secondary is a particular example of this (see National Languages Strategy, DfES 2002), but it equally applies from year to year and teacher to teacher within school.

Reflection Task

Evaluating your mark book

Look at your mark book for one particular class. What exactly have you recorded for each skill? What picture does it enable you to give for each pupil? What does it tell you about your teaching? What could someone understand immediately by looking at it? How does it record and show learners' progress?

Good practice in assessment provides essential underpinning for effective learning. Features of such good practice include clear policies delivered through practical procedures, such as regular marking; continuous feedback to pupils on both oral and written performance in MFL; target-setting based on meticulous record-keeping; analysis of a range of evidence and data; the involvement of pupils in assessment; and the use of this information to inform the planning of sequences of lessons. (OFSTED 2002a)

What needs to be known about learners and their achievements?

Different audiences require different information about individual pupils and groups of pupils. The chart on p40 sets out who needs what information. Background information will be required by some audiences, while others will be far more interested in a learner's current progress and achievement. Some audiences will require both types of information, for example the class teacher. For many recipients, the information can and should be anonymous, but others need specific knowledge on named individuals.

Trainee/NQT Task

Who needs assessment information?

• Consider what the requirements of each of the audiences in the chart below might be in relation to pupils you teach.

• Decide which of the audiences would need which information, if any, from you and your records on an individual learner.

• Connect the two boxes in the chart with the appropriate audiences as in the example.

• How many audiences need to have both types of information?

• What could you provide based on your current assessment and recording systems?

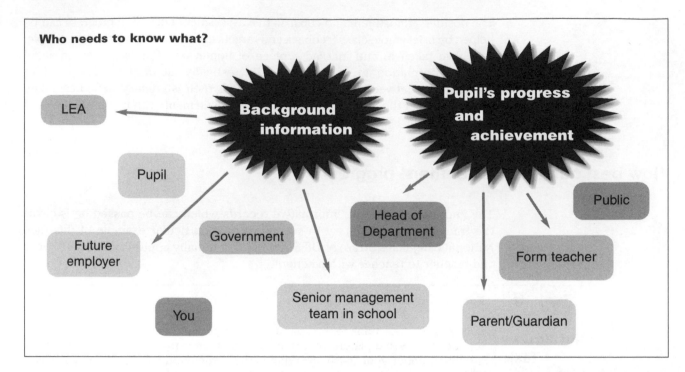

Who needs to know what?

- LEA
- Background information
- Pupil's progress and achievement
- Pupil
- Public
- Head of Department
- Future employer
- Government
- Form teacher
- You
- Senior management team in school
- Parent/Guardian

When assessing and recording therefore, the requirements of each audience have to be borne in mind. Some information needs to be collected and recorded by individual teachers, other items on a departmental basis and some at a whole school level.

Your 'mark book'

Most schools now have pupil data available electronically – make the most of this and download as much as necessary to make your mark 'book' as helpful as you can. This might include photographs, background information, etc. Many schools issue staff with pre-prepared class lists, which you can then tailor electronically to suit your needs. Perhaps a mixture of electronic recording and entering grades/comments by hand may work best. Many schools have now adopted electronic means of recording attendance and other information – any recording system needs to fit in of course with the whole school system. It needs to be a system that is **used** and which is understood throughout the department or it becomes meaningless.

The following section looks at how a 'mark book' could be organised, whether the markbook uses ICT (e.g. Excel spreadsheets) or is hand written in the traditional teacher's planner or mark book. The mark book is divided into different categories of information, depending on its purpose and how often it is required. Background information in a mark book; information to be entered every lesson; and information to be entered regularly.

Background information

This information is recorded usually once a year only and then used for reference, although of course if pupils move sets, or year groups are placed into sets at a particular point in the year, this information would need to be re-collected.

Basic information to access and/or record for each learner consists of:

- name (note also surname of parent/guardian in case of telephone calls and for parents' evenings, etc);
- date of birth;
- form group/form tutor (where class not taught in form groups);
- information such as CAT (Cognitive Ability Test) scores, reading ages, etc;
- latest NC levels (as appropriate);
- predicted grades (as appropriate);
- SEN/individual education plans;
- latest test/assessment results;
- agreed targets (e.g. minimum target calculated via data analysis by school's assessment co-ordinator – see Chapter 6).

Ideally some information in this category can be produced via the school's database and accessed/downloaded/printed by individual teachers.

Information to be entered every lesson

Information that is to be recorded every lesson (where appropriate) consists of:

- attendance;
- punctuality;
- remembered/forgotten equipment;
- merits/sanctions.

The teacher should be able to enter information in this category quickly and concisely, but the information must also be meaningful. For example, an oblique stroke for attendance could be supplemented by 'L' for late, '!' for forgotten equipment, 'M' for merit or 'D' for detention. The symbols are obviously to a great extent arbitrary, but must be understood by anyone who will use the information. One square in the mark book can in this way yield a lot of useful information, and patterns become clear.

Head of Department Task

Recording symbols and systems

- If you are a new Head of Department or feel there is varying practice across the department, find out what codes, symbols and systems are used by each member of the department.
- Decide whether there would be an advantage in having an agreed system.

Information to be entered regularly

Information to be recorded regularly (according to departmental policy) includes:

- class marks/responses for each Attainment Target (AT);
- homework completion/marks/responses for each AT;
- results of tests/formal assessments;
- vocabulary test results;
- other marks, e.g. any ICT-based or independent activities.

For each mark in this category, it needs to be clear what exactly the mark was for, what the raw score was out of, what the task was, etc. The column heading should therefore contain this information with the date, possible marks available, precise reference to worksheet/textbook/test etc. This is important – if it is not clear what the mark was for, a raw score of '8' will not mean very much after a few weeks have elapsed.

A separate page or colour coding for each AT demonstrates quickly whether all four skills are being assessed and how pupils are progressing within each one.

Recording in this category can also easily incorporate **differentiation**, using two or more adjacent columns for a task. For example, **all** pupils would be given a mark recorded for a core task. Those who attempt another task would be given a **separate** mark. This is because to combine the marks would lead to a skewed picture of achievement. For example, if in a listening task the questions everybody was expected to answer were marked out of ten, but there was then a bonus 'challenge' type question worth five further marks, the first column should only record everybody's mark out of ten; the second column will record the mark of those pupils who attempted the bonus question. This gives a clear picture of each pupil's achievement, e.g. 7 + 3, 10 + 0, 5 + 5, etc, but it can also be helpful to see which pupils **tried** the challenge, even if they did not gain any marks. This system can also be used for indicating if a pupil used support material for example.

Other information

ICT software (e.g. CD-ROMs, on-line and Web-based materials such as **quia.com** and **Hot Potatoes**) can be used for self/teacher/'objective' assessment and (limited) feedback. Much of this is, of course, restricted in its scope, but can nevertheless be useful. Data from pupils' attempts at a vocabulary exercise using **quia.com** could inform a teacher quickly about areas where they struggled, but proper analysis is necessary to provide real feedback to learners and to inform teachers and departments fully. The National Languages Strategy, for example (DfES 2002: 39), proposes that ICT will be used so learners can self-assess before formal assessment.

Maintaining a page where more 'prose-like' information can be recorded is helpful, or even an exercise book per class with a page for each pupil. Information suitable for this section would be comments on reports; agreed targets at pupil review sessions; relevant extra personal information such as coursework topic, work experience placement: whatever is relevant to the particular group. Other information in this section might include any contact with home, particular strengths of pupil – perhaps participation in extra curricular MFL activities etc.

This type of information demands more time of course: if ICT is used for writing reports, then the reproduction of such information for your own records is much easier.

Some schools have taken this idea further, and have developed **class folders**. These consist of a ring binder for each class, with a plastic wallet for each pupil. The file builds up during the year or the key stage, and if a learner moves groups, their individual folder moves with them. The contents of the folders may include the following items:

- pupil self-assessment sheets (see Chapter 4);
- target-setting documentation (see Chapter 4);
- formal assessments and results;
- feedback sheets on oral presentations;
- copies of reports;
- actual test papers – marked and with comments.

Although this could appear bureaucratic, causing extra paperwork, it has proved very helpful for learners as they are able to see their progress and make sense of comments. They see their targets in a more coherent context. When the class are completing their self-assessments, pupils will have their file to review, add to, etc. The National Languages Strategy (DfES 2002) proposes that 'small steps of achievement will be recognised at beginner level to provide a motivator for continued learning.' 'The descriptors will take the form of simple, positive 'I can' statements.'

Trainee/NQT Task

Analysis of a mark book

- Ask to look at the mark book of your mentor or other experienced teacher. Alternatively use the examples provided on pp44–46.

- What information can be gained on each pupil?

- What indication is gained of their strengths and weaknesses?

For examples of mark book pages, see the samples on pp44–46 from Joan Hughes of Studley High School and Marianne Tchakhotine of Henley in Arden High School. Pupils' names have been removed.

Joan's comments on her use of her mark book: 'I take books in fortnightly and mark a whole section, bearing in mind how the pupil has responded in the lessons. My mark accompanied by a detailed comment in their exercise book will acknowledge all four skills, effort, presentation and homeworks completed. The mark in my book is out of 20, and I aim to encourage rather than to stifle effort and enjoyment. The mark tells me whether a pupil is keeping up with all the work set, if he or she has been absent etc. Lines across indicate absence but a blank space shows that the book was not handed in. I record statistics next to names, reminding me of a pupil's expected performance and any learning difficulties. The mark book also contains end of module test results, with all information recorded on a pupil's own results sheet. The examples here show a sheet from the mark book for a top set Year 9 group, with their CATs score and their reading age followed by a range of marks. The second sheet is the end of module test results for the same group.'

Marianne's records are very detailed and informative. Her seating plan for her Year 7 class for example indicates not only who sits where, but also vital brief information such as whether a pupil is dyslexic. This provides immediately visible information **during** as well as pre- and post- lessons. Marianne then has a page of background information on each pupil, with details such as form, book, number, any special needs, date of birth and reading age. For years other than Year 7, this includes also, for example, the previous year's exam results and predicted or target grades. She records merits, detentions, homework 'red marks' and effort grades. Particularly interesting is the fact she records the pupils' **own** targets (the third of the three mark sheets shown). Some of these are very specific, e.g. 'Have more than 84% in the next assessment' and are very useful as part of an ongoing dialogue between teacher and pupil. Marianne makes specific comments in her mark book to mention at parents' evening, including comments for example on whether a pupil forgets books frequently as well as remarks on class participation. This helps create a fuller picture when combined with detailed records of test results, class and homework marks in all four skills.

Record keeping of this detail does take time to set up – mark books need to be organised and set out carefully so pages are available for all necessary information – but the 'pay back' is substantial:

■ providing information and tracking pupils' achievement is much more straightforward;

■ evidence for an individual teacher's professional development is readily available.

The crucial element of both Marianne's and Joan's record keeping is that it serves a purpose – it does far more than fill some boxes on a page.

Subject: **French**

Group: **9G1.**

No.	NAMES	MARKS	N FER	R4	Dt	Module 7 4.9.02	11.9.02	16.9.02	23.9.02	8.11.02	19.11.02		Module 8 15.11.03	22.1.03			
RT			102	13	29	18	18	19	14	17	/		10	16			
PXS			105	12	27×	19	18	17		17	/		15	18			
DJ			101	12	29	/	17	16	14	18			/	15			
DJ			101	15	31	19	18	19	19	19	/		14	18			
RT			94	14	27×	19	19	18	19	17	✓		12	17			
DJ			108	13	29	18	16	19	17	16	/		13	17			
RT			84	15	29	19	20	20	20	19	/		14	19			
PXS			109	13	29	19	19	20	19	19	/		17	18			
RH			121	12	/	19	18	20	20	19	/		17	20			
RH			120	15	33	19	19	19	18	19	19	/	/				
CB			122	12	31	17	19	20		19			17	18			
PXS			109	15	33	18	17	17	17	18	19	/	14	14			
RH			114	12	27×	15	16	18	19	17			10	18			
RH						18	18	20	18	19	17	/	13	16			
PXS			99	12	29	19	18	15	16	16		/	14				
PXS			131	12	31	19	19	17	18	18		✓	13	19			
RH			117	12	33	19	19	15	18	17	18		14	19			
CB			132	14	31	20	20	20	20	19		/	20	18			
RH						19	17	18	18	16		/	11	16			
PXS			116	14	27×	18	19	20	19	19		✓	17	20			
CB			107	12	25××	18	18	18	19	19	18	/	16	16			
PXS			100	13	31	19	19	18	16	16	16	✓	15	14			
DJ			95	14	31	19	19	18	18	18			11	18			
CB			122	13	27×	19	19	18	18	18	18		9	17			
RT			104	12	31	18	18	18	17	16	17	/		16			
DJ			118	14	31	20	19	17	20	18			18	17			
RT			112	13	31	19	18	19	19	18		/	12	18			
CB			105	15	31	/	20	20	17	19		/	14	17			
PXS			100	15	31	20	20	20	16	N		/	16	18			
PXS			114	13	31	20	18	19	20	19		/	16	19			
RH			121	12	29	19	18	18	18	18			15	19			
RH			121	13	29	19	19	20	19	18		/	15	17			

Source: Studley High School

	A	B	C	D	E	F	G	H	I	J	K	L	M	N
1														
2														
3	Controle 7: Jour J													
4	Subject French	Group 9G1					Date NOV. 2002							
5		AT				Gra	Total	%		KS3 Level				Total
6	Pupil	1	2	3	4				Display. (ALL)	1	2	3	4	Level
7	28	24		32	20.	10.	86.							
8														
9					16.	7.	23/130	77.	✓				5	
10		20½		26		10.	56½/66	86		4		4		4
11		16½		18	16	7.	57½	67	✓	4		4	5	4+
12		23		28	19	9.	79.	92	✓ ✓	5		5	5	5
13		20½		25	17.	7.	69½	81	✓ ✓	4+		4+	5	4+
14		20		20	11	7½	58½	68		4		4	4	4
15		22		26	18½	9	75½	88	✓ ✓	5		5	5	5
16		22		26	19	10	77.	89		5		4+	5	5
17		21½		25	19	10.	75½	88	✓	5		4+	5	5
18		22		27	18	10.	70	81	✓	5		4+	5	5
19		19½		26	15	10.	70½	82	✓ ✓	4+		4	5	4+
20		17		20	18.	10.	65	76	✓ ✓	4		4	5	4+
21		18½		16	18	7.	59½	69.		4		3	5	
22		21½		24	19	8½	73	85		5		4	5	5.
23				20	16.	6.	~~42/130~~	~~73~~	42/62 68			4	5	4+
24		22		24	18	10.	74	86	✓ ✓	5		4	5	5
25		19		26	19	9	73	85	✓ ✓	4+		5		
26		22		26	20.	9	77	89	✓ ✓	5		4+	5	5
27		18½		16	12	10	56½	66		4		3	4	
28		22		28	19	10.	79.	92.	✓	4+		5	5	5
29				22	17	8½	47½/62	77				4	5	4+
30		17		22	19	9	67	78	✓ ✓	4		4	5	
31		15		14	19	8	56	65	✓	4		3	5	4+
32		18½		25	19	7	69½	81		4		4+	5	4+
33		19		24	16	7	66.	77		4		4+	5	4+
34		17		26	19	10	72	84		4		5	5	5
35		17		25	15	8	65	76	✓	4		4+	5	4+
36		23		22	19	10	74	86.		5		4+	5	5
37		22		22	19.	9.	72	84	✓ ✓	5		4+	5	5
38		22½		27	17	10.	76½	89	✓ ✓	5		4+	5	5
39		16		14	12	9½	51½	60	✓ ✓	4		3	4	4
40		21½		28	19	9.	77½	90.	✓ ✓	4+		5	5	5
41														
42								0						
43														
44	Year Average %	73%.												
45														
46	Group av %	81%.												
47														
48														
49														
50														
51														
52														
53														
54														

Source: Studley High School

Pupils' Targets

Be in top of the set

Improve writing /spelling – move up.

Speak well / improve writing / go to France go on an exchange

Write letters / speak better / go on an exchange

Move up set / be able to speak to people / understand French / write

Speak fluently French at end of Y11 / improve writing

Have more than 84% next assess / improve list & sp. / Good GCSE

Be more confidente / Do well in tests / Top for French.

Have lots of merits / move up / speak well at end of GCSE /

Be top of the set / Improve speaking – writing / Have many merits.

Do well in GCSE / speak well to go on trips.

Be more confident / answer more questions / speak better / spell better

Be fluent in French by the end of Y11.

Be good to go on an exchange / move up set / Improve list / speak fluently

Speak fluently by Y11 / Improve my writing / Keep enjoying French

Speak fluently by Y11 / Get high marks in tests / Have more merits

Learn more vocab / speak well to go on an exchange / Improve spelling

Improve Writing / List / speak.

Move up set / Improve spelling / Revise more / Improve speaking.

Get good marks in tests / be able to speak to French people / Improve learning

Be more confident to speak / not rush in my work / move up set

Improve spelling / speak fluently to go to Paris / Good grade at GCSE

Improve grades / work neatly / speak with confident / spend more time learning

Speak fluently by the end of Y11 / Write properly / be neater / move set

Get more merits / learn harder / Get better grades / move up set / go to France speak to French people

Be more confident in speaking /

Use French in my job / speak fluently quickly / move up set.

Speak fluently A.S.A.P. / Improve list / spelling.

Source: Henley in Arden High School

Making assessment work – practicalities

Developing the department's assessment policies and practices

Any assessment policies need of course to be seen alongside schemes of work and to be integrated into them. As a new Head of Department or in a situation where, for example, there has been substantial staff turnover, or leading up to or following an inspection or review, it would be beneficial to use one or more of the following activities to assess how processes and performance could be improved.

Below are some ideas to help a department think about, adapt and develop their assessment practices. A Head of Department needs to evaluate the department's current position, and to decide which activity would be most suitable at the moment.

Departmental Task

Collecting together the department's assessment toolkit

- **Activity type:** collection of materials/support.

- **Suitable for:** Heads of Department wishing to ensure they are fully informed on assessment, and as preparation for assessment policy and practice development.

The list below contains useful information and support necessary for the departmental toolkit. The toolkit should help members of the department to use assessment more effectively, confidently and from a more informed perspective. Some information should be contained in the departmental handbook, some referred to in the assessment policy and cross-referenced in the schemes of work.

> **A departmental toolkit for assessment could comprise:**
>
> - school and departmental policy on assessment;
> - schemes of work with key assessment and moderation tasks highlighted;
> - National Curriculum and Level Descriptions (including pupil-friendly level descriptors – see Chapter 5);
> - Programme of Study (and grid – see Chapter 2);
> - QCA and National Curriculum support materials, including from their websites at **www.qca.org.uk** and **www.nc.uk.net** (e.g. schemes of work at KS2 and KS3, Exemplification of Standards material);
> - GCSE, AS/A level and other specifications and examiners' reports: filed by year and language, alongside copies of examination papers in all skills;
> - student-friendly or annotated versions of the GCSE or A level marking criteria (see Chapter 5);
> - support and advice material available from Examining Groups, including from their websites (**www.edexcel.org.uk**, **www.ocr.org.uk**, **www.neab.ac.uk**);
> - moderation examples collated and discussed as a department (both for external course work and internal key assessments);
> - model mark schemes, reports;
> - OFSTED reports: national and school-based (see **www.ofsted.gov.uk**);
> - other relevant information (e.g. the assessment information from the National Languages Strategy (DfES 2002), and Common European Framework levels for assessing language proficiency **www.dialang.org**, Council of Europe Draft 2 Framework, Modern Languages: Learning, teaching, assessment, a common European framework of reference (1998) – using the European Language Portfolio; see Chapter 6, p116);
> - references to relevant publications, statistics and reference materials.

**Departmental
Task** **2**

Starting from a clean slate

- **Activity type:** discussion/reflection.
- **Suitable for:** departmental meeting/teachers' day.
- **Needed when:** the department wishes to re-consider what assessment involves; perhaps in a department with a new HoD or where there has been considerable staff turnover. It would also be useful in a department which has recently been inspected by OFSTED and where assessment issues were highlighted.
- **Could incorporate:** INSET/ITE Task 3 in Chapter 7, p129.

Ensure everyone in the department has seen the following questions at least a week before they are due to be discussed as a department, and that they have a copy of any existing departmental assessment policies and OFSTED reports where appropriate:

- What is assessment?
- How do **you** assess and monitor learners' progress?
- What do you want assessment to **do**?
- What would a successful assessment policy look like in **this** department?
- Does the department need to think about some fundamental changes to its assessment policy?

During the discussion make notes on what issues are being raised and make some concrete decisions about:

- what should happen next (consider setting dates for some of the activities outlined below);
- who will take responsibility for what;
- whether any school or external support for implementation of any decisions is required.

**Departmental
Task** **3**

Setting minimum expectations (marking, testing, homework)

- **Activity type:** discussion/reflection.
- **Suitable for:** departmental meeting.
- **Needed when:** the department is finalising or adapting its assessment policy.
- **Could incorporate:** Minimum assessment expectations, p66.

Ensure everyone in the department has a copy of the draft or existing assessment policy. Give every member of staff a copy of the minimum expectations grid on p49 (adapted as appropriate for your department: a template is available on the website – see Web template 4) a week before the meeting. They should complete it from their perspective before group discussion at the meeting. '…' indicates a time, e.g. every two weeks, every day, etc.

During the discussion, have an OHT version or A3 size version of the minimum expectations grid and add comments and notes where appropriate. This copy can be pinned on the office wall after the meeting for further comments where necessary.

Decisions need to be made regarding at least the following:

- When will the final version be decided upon?
- How will we know expectations are being met?
- Do you need any school or external support for implementation?

Assessment in our department: what should be our minimum expectations?			
	KS3	KS4	Post-16
Collect and mark each learner's exercise book/class work every …			
Set learning homework every …			
Set written homework every …			
Set individual targets with learners every …			
Conduct a formal assessment in all four ATs every …			
Carry out pupil reviews every …			
Evaluate a lesson from your own teaching perspective in detail every …			

 4

Departmental Task

Evaluating your own teaching and teaching across the department

- **Activity type:** investigation/collation of information/reflection.

- **Suitable for:** completion over half a term before an appraisal meeting or training day.

- **Needed when:** members of the department need to look at how planning, teaching, learning and assessment are inter-linked, where there are particular strengths and where improvements might be required.

> Ensure everyone in the department has a copy of the evaluation template (see p24 or Web template 2) (adapted as appropriate). This could be made available electronically. Teachers in the department then receive the following plan of action, where timescale and parameters suit the particular circumstances:
>
> - Choose at least three of your groups to evaluate your teaching. Please include different abilities and key stages, and if possible, one more challenging group.
> - Use the evaluation pro forma with at least three different classes for at least one lesson per class during this half term.
> - Bring your evaluations to the meeting/training session on (date) or use them as appropriate in your appraisal/induction meetings/threshold applications.
> - What issues regarding learning and assessment emerge from your evaluations?

5

Departmental Task

Evaluating a set of exercise books

- **Activity type:** investigation.

- **Suitable for:** after a few weeks of an NQT's or GTP's first term, or midway through a trainee's placement.

- **Needed when:** it is necessary to look in detail at the overall picture of a class to establish progress and consider assessment issues.

- **Could incorporate:** Suggestions in Chapters 4 and 5 for marking and responding to pupils' work; INSET/ITE Task 7 (p135) in Chapter 7.

The teacher or trainee should be given this task a week before you (or the induction tutor) would like to discuss it.

- Choose a class you have had responsibility for over at least four weeks.
- Evaluate their exercise books critically, looking at class work, homework.
- Relate your thoughts to the pupils' contributions in class.

You might look at issues similar to those outlined below, for example looking at a set of Year 9 class exercise books might yield the following information about the pupils:

- their performance in their homework;
- their performance in tasks set in class;
- their effectiveness at organising their work, using their own learning strategies, making notes from information given, setting their work out in a clear and usable manner;
- the above elements in relation to their oral contributions in class;
- identifying common errors to highlight which areas of grammar they had particular problems with.

The teacher or trainee should discuss findings with (name) on (date) and should be prepared to answer the following questions:

- What have you learnt about the learning and progress of this group in the four skills?
- Did anything surprise you?
- What do you need to do now?
- Do you require any support with the implementation of your ideas?

6

Departmental Task

Auditing departmental practices

- **Activity type:** investigation.

- **Suitable for:** when a Head of Department wishes to find out what happens within the department regarding a specific assessment practice (e.g. vocabulary testing)

- **Needed when:** strengths and areas for improvement need to be identified and shared; leading up to or following on from an inspection; before developing departmental policies

- **Could incorporate:** the departmental audit template illustrated below (see also Web template 5 below), which could be adapted for other topics as appropriate (for example, using some of the homework ideas further on in this chapter, see p54).

> Departmental 'audits' can be useful for a Head of Department to:
>
> - raise awareness amongst staff in the department of what they could/should/must do;
> - analyse strengths in the department and therefore enable the HoD to illustrate good practice;
> - highlight trends and gaps in departmental practice.
>
> Examples where you as HoD might wish to use an audit might include:
>
> - coverage of programme of study (see p30 or Web template 3).
> - possible NC levels to be achieved in homework tasks, for example, some tasks restrict achievement to e.g. Level 4;
> - as part of classroom observation with colleagues, e.g. what types of questions used, etc.

 Web template 5

Departmental audit template

Homework activity (please add further examples as appropriate)	Year Group/frequency of use during January to March		
	Year 7	Year 8	Year 9
Learning vocabulary			
Worksheet: matching			
Worksheet: gap fill			
Puzzle/game			
Summary of grammar point			
Recording on cassette			
Listing learning strategies			
Dictionary work			
Reading *preparation*			
Memorising a short text			

7

Departmental Task

Moderation across and between languages in the department

- **Activity type:** marking, comparison and discussion.
- **Suitable for:** a training day.
- **Needed when:** the department wishes to produce moderation material and to improve assessment consistency.
- **Could incorporate:** procedure for marking checklist (below).

A few weeks before the training day:

- ask members of the department to select one piece of work from each class they teach;
- each piece is copied twice – once unmarked, once marked.

Preparation for the day:

- the HoD copies each unmarked piece of work for every member of the department, along with mark schemes/criteria/other reference and support materials (see assessment toolkit, page 47), together with the context as appropriate (for example, year group, set);
- the work is then marked in pairs and results compared;
- outcomes can form a moderation reference for the department's assessment policy/examples.

General procedure for marking (see Chapter 4 for further details):

- ensure everyone understands the criteria;
- work is then marked against criteria;
- feedback refers to criteria;
- understandable targets are set and monitored.

Raising standards of effective assessment across the department

Of the following suggestions for raising standards of effective assessment across the department, many can be tailored to a format similar to those of Departmental Tasks 1–7 above.

- Involve trainee teachers and NQTs in joint marking with more experienced teachers, e.g. swap class sets of tests/exercise books.
- Pair up members of the department to 'shadow' a few oral examinations.
- Pair up members of the department for parents' evening – less experienced with more experienced (see also Chapter 6 and Chapter 7, INSET/ITE Task 6, p134).
- If you have a departmental 'space', post up a different marked task (class or homework) each week with the mark scheme etc.
- Set trainees and NQTs a specific AT to assess in one particular week. Ask them to provide an example for each class of how they assessed that skill.
- Provide an initial list which is then developed at a departmental meeting of how to 'test' for understanding in class without expecting translation into English.
- Use 'tests' as a theme for a department meeting (even a vocabulary test could fulfil this function). Ask the department: What were you testing? What did you say to the pupils about the test? Did you give them any specific advice? What was the timescale (e.g. did you set it on Monday and test on Wednesday)? How did you devise the mark scheme? How did you inform the pupils of the mark scheme and criteria? Who marked it, when and how? Where and how did you record the marks? What did you and the pupils do with the marks?

- Key area for MFL – fluency/accuracy. Ask members of the department to consider different types of task and whether they are primarily assessing for fluency or accuracy in each one. Is it made clear to the pupils each time which area is taking priority? Example: in a quick-fire repetition task, it may be pronunciation that takes precedence, but in a team game on the interactive whiteboard spelling is clearly crucial.
- A department could build up some suggestions as to where and how pupils can do extra work on a vocabulary field, grammar point, etc, ideally ICT-based, perhaps on the school Intranet.

Homework

The following quotes are a selection of views pupils gave when asked about their MFL homework.

 *My homework in Modern Foreign Languages is ...*

- *good so we can get good grades. (Girl, 13)*
- *very helpful – gives me an idea of how good I am. (Girl, 15)*
- *good depending on the lesson we had before, like what the lesson was about. (Girl, 12)*
- *brilliant because it's already been explained. (Girl, 12)*
- *we have to write things down to do with verbs. (Boy, 13)*
- *medium hard because our teacher combines the lesson and in the past. (Boy, 12)*
- *sometimes puzzling but it helps me learn. (Girl, 12)*
- *quite difficult, but understandable. (Girl, 14)*
- *to see what I have learnt. (Girl, 13)*
- *to practise and learn grammar and vocabulary given in lessons. (Girl, 15)*
- *good to recap the class work in the day. (Girl, 15)*
- *difficult but useful (if done). (Girl, 14)*
- *quite useful but I don't like homework. (Boy, 15)*
- *fairly hard because if you can't remember the work very well, you don't have anything to look it up in. (Girl, 15)*
- *hard but it helps you to look up new words. (Boy, 15)*
- *easy, as I'm able to use a dictionary for help. (Girl, 15)*
- *hard because I forget what it means. (Girl, 13)*

 8

Trainee/NQT Task

Experience of homework

- What experience have you had of homework so far (types, etc)?
- What do you feel are the reasons for/benefits of homework?
- Have you found it is set appropriately and regularly according to agreed procedures?
- What exactly are valid homework activities?

9

Trainee/NQT Task

Homework policy and practice

- What is the homework policy/schedule of your school and your department?
- How have you implemented it so far into your own planning and assessment?
- What have you found most beneficial and what most problematic?
- After reading the pupils' comments on p53, consider what your pupils might say about homework you've set recently.

The reasons for giving homework are extensive (see for example Nicholls, 1999). There is also substantial information at **www.dfee.gov.uk/homework,** where as well as outlining purposes of homework, advice is available on feedback, recommended time to be spent on homework and ways of making the system manageable.

Many of the arguments in favour of homework include such ideas as promoting learners' independence, extending learning beyond the classroom, encouraging further research/investigation, providing information about learners' progress. If you consider the homework you have set recently, how many of these goals would have been met?

Suggested homework tasks should be built into schemes of work and certain tasks highlighted as key pieces of work, which should be attempted by all pupils. Flexibility for individual teachers to set their own versions of homework should of course be there, but there should be enough ideas and recommendations in the scheme of work that no teacher is left wondering what could be appropriate. If certain homework tasks are identified as key, then comparisons become easier.

As a department, an audit of homework types (see Departmental Task 6 on p51) could be very helpful to establish current practice. Results could then be collated and added to. The list below could be adapted with other ideas to form the audit.

There is a wide range of possible types of homework, catering for a variety of learning styles and covering all skills. The list below includes some less widely seen suggestions.

Homework ideas

- Pupils summarise a grammar point.
- Occasionally give pupils a choice for homework completion, e.g. record the presentation on cassette or write it out or do it on PowerPoint etc.
- Pupils list five ways they have used to memorise vocabulary.
- Review of a TV programme/book/film using a framework, where each pupil completes one a term to be displayed.
- Look up a set of new words in the dictionary and record appropriately.
- Read a text and annotate it with words related to English/which they know/which they don't know, etc.
- Write in English the phrases they feel would be crucial in a particular context as preparation for a new topic.
- Submit homework as an e-mail attachment.
- Memorise a short text or poem.
- Devise a mnemonic for a grammar rule or list of vocabulary.

- Language challenge, e.g. create as many words as possible from one target language phrase.
- Web-based activities/research.
- Logic puzzles, where reading and thinking are paramount rather than writing.
- Devise language puzzles and games for a different (perhaps younger) class.

Homework tips

Some of the following tips on homework could perhaps be adapted for a departmental handbook.

- Giving homework is a vital part of your lesson planning. Refer to the schemes of work.
- Think carefully about homework when you are planning your lessons. Make sure you provide an appropriate activity, building on work done in the lesson. Think about when to set it, give clear instructions, and a range of homeworks over time.
- Make the setting of homework a priority in the lesson, e.g. work over in detail what is to be drafted or written up at home.
- Don't give pupils homework activities to do in class and trivial things to do at home.
- Don't just give a 'cop-out' homework, such as 'Make sure you know all the vocabulary we did today.'
- Homework shouldn't just be given for the sake of it.
- Check that homework is still going to be appropriate if you don't get through your lesson plan. Some homeworks are very dependent on progress in the lesson, others more 'stand alone'.
- Put yourself in the position of the pupils – would **you** want to do this homework, or are you just setting it because you have to?
- Consider providing pupils with hints on how to do homework.
- Homework should be within the ability of the pupil, but also provide some opportunity of 'stretching'.
- What forms of homework? Learning, written, exercise, 'investigation', completion of work begun in class (disadvantages – slower pupils have more to do, faster pupils have no challenge, encourages rushing), project type work, reading work, etc.
- Check that you know the school's homework policy. Do pupils at your school have a homework diary? You need to get into whatever system is used. Is there a homework schedule when, for example, French can only be set on certain nights?
- When should homework be collected? At the beginning of the lesson? At the end? How often do you take pupils' books in?
- Homework – and the manner in which it is handled – is a good opportunity to teach pupils social and organisational skills as well as a body of knowledge.
- Be careful if setting homework which requires a pupil to work with words unknown to them (in KS3 especially), i.e. unheard in class.
- Consider backing up homework instructions with written instructions on board.
- If the same mistakes come up in many homeworks, this tells you something about your teaching or the task!
- Go over the main problems in class.
- When setting homework, give clear instructions and a demonstration. Check that everyone understands what they are to do.
- Always test learning homeworks – otherwise no-one will bother learning it all!

Homework policies for a department

Again, back to basics – why do homework? Reasons should be explicit on the policy, and enacted in real life. Is it:

- to give pupils opportunities to consolidate/improve/extend their classroom learning?
- to enable pupils to carry out work which would not be possible in class time?
- to give them practice in time management and meeting deadlines?
- to allow pupils a chance to use their preferred way of, for example, memorising vocabulary?

Have a look at the Homework advice below from Tile Hill Wood School and Language College. This is a section from the school's department handbook:

Homework in Modern Foreign Languages

- Through the use of homework we aim to extend learning beyond school.

- A range of homework tasks which are integral to the topic is included in the schemes of work for KS3. It is desirable to achieve a balance in the type of homework set: learning vocabulary/key phrases, written exercises, reading tasks, 'prepare to say' as in oral presentations and role plays, draft paragraphs for coursework for example, research in the Library or on the Internet, use of a piece of software in the Open Language Centre, etc.

- It is also important to take into account the level of the class and the ability of the individual in order to set realistic homework. Differentiation will often happen by outcome but sometimes a differentiated task is required, e.g. a modified exercise with a help sheet.

- The homework timetable for years 7–9 should be adhered to. As a guide, each homework should last roughly 30 minutes in KS3. Adequate time should be devoted to the setting of homework in class. It is school policy to write homework on the board, explain clearly and check that students have noted it down clearly in study planners. It is advisable to walk round and check quickly that students have noted homework as requested.

- At KS4 there is no set homework timetable as oral presentations, coursework assignments may be set over a longer period. It is equally important that homework is noted carefully by students. It is vital that they are made aware of exam requirements and note key deadlines and exam dates in their study planners. Overdue coursework is to be chased; there is a whole school check before parents' evening in Year 10.

- Follow-up to homework is important and will include discussion in class with follow-up exercises in the next/subsequent lessons, displays of work, regular and prompt marking with written guidance where relevant, oral/written testing of learning homeworks, etc. A class could occasionally be asked to provide evidence of learning, e.g. self-produced games such as dominoes, picture/word cards, wordsearches, test/teach a parent, etc.

- Commendations, stickers and praise for good work are common features. When particularly pleasing work has been achieved, please send student with the work to the HoD. Similarly, missing or overdue homework should be followed up, noting problems on the attendance slips to alert tutors and year heads. Students should be asked to complete late work for the next lesson and where necessary a lunchtime detention if they fail to catch up. If the problem persists, please alert the HoD. An after-school detention with a letter home can be issued and discussion take place with the Year Head.

Source: Tile Hill Wood School and Language College

Vocabulary learning and testing

Classroom tests are a quick and efficient way of testing recall of simple facts (e.g. FL vocabulary) and basic skills (e.g. spelling). (Stobart & Gipps, 1997: 22)

6

Reflection
Task

Vocabulary

- What vocabulary and structures exactly do you wish pupils to learn (single items, phrases, parts of the verb, idioms, topic-based, function-based groupings)?

- What does it mean to **know** vocabulary (meaning/pronunciation/spelling; receptive/productive – and how to use it)?

- How will you encourage learners to link sound and spelling/written word?

- Vocabulary books: systematic recording – how will you teach pupils to do this?

- What vocabulary do you want them to **know** and **use** by the end of a lesson/a unit?

- How will you record marks of tests, e.g. vocabulary, verbs, grammatical structures, etc?

- Vocabulary tests – do they always have to be written?

Practising, testing and learning vocabulary

The following ideas and suggestions for practising, testing and learning vocabulary have been used by University of Warwick Partnership School teachers and trainees over a number of years.

Learning vocabulary

- look/cover/say;
- mnemonics;
- rewrite in different order;
- pupils grade words themselves (easy/known; middle; difficult);
- categorise into two lists: items understood/items to be looked up later;
- spend a couple of minutes in class practising out loud;
- make a little book – A4 paper folded into eight, torn and flicked over;
- colour coding;
- use squared paper and create blocks of words with same endings, e.g. professions in French ending in *-er, -ier, -eur,* etc, so pupils start to see patterns.

Practising vocabulary

- reverse bingo – the winner is the one with one picture left – teacher calls out, e.g. nineteen of the twenty words;
- anagrams, matching half words, *Fun With Texts,* etc.;
- codes – dictate the numbers which they write down – they then crack the code according to a list;
- write words down – missing all vowels or missing first/last letters – they must complete them;
- at the end of a topic give them the alphabet – they must try and fill in a word for each letter relating to the topic;
- a good way of consolidating previous vocabulary is to prepare an OHT divided into twelve mini pictures: all the usual activities can be used to establish how well the pupils recognise and know, and can use the items. For example, you repeat, they repeat, then repeat only if it's the right one, play match three, combine two or more mini-pictures to create a sentence/phrase, etc;
- flashcards of **words** can be played with in the same way as flashcards of pictures, i.e. quick flash, revelation, guess the card etc;

■ pupils use new words to make puzzles, e.g. anagrams, crosswords, wordsearch, hangman, etc.

Testing vocabulary

■ Pupils work from a pre-printed sheet for vocabulary tests which can then be stuck in books (see the example below).
■ Produce a chart for pupils to make a graph of their vocabulary test scores. Pupils can then follow up their scores and make them worth something. Recording vocabulary results can be done using Excel, and pupil-friendly graphs and targets produced.
■ Vocabulary test by Blockbusters.
■ Differentiate or tailor-make your vocabulary tests, e.g. first three always from the target language to English; the second three always English to the target language, but less emphasis on accuracy; the last four from English to the target language with accuracy very important.

Example of a pre-printed vocabulary test sheet

Name:		Datum:	
Schulfächer			
Englisch		**Deutsch**	
1		Chemie	
2		Sozialwissenschaften	
3		Kochen	
4		Französisch	
5		Textilgestaltung	
6	music		
7	history		
8	English		
9	geography		
10	maths		
BONUS! The German for Economics is: W_____			

Source: Elly Crofton, Coundon Court School

Key points	■ To make assessment more effective in order to improve pupils' learning and achievements, it must be consistent and above all used.
	■ Monitoring and recording pupils' progress should be a constructive process which helps all parties understand and improve pupils' learning and not an empty exercise of writing down meaningless data.

4

Responding to pupils' work effectively

Marking, feedback, target setting, pupil self-assessment and review

Marking pupils' work is an accepted routine aspect of a teacher's role. Yet, marking needs to be much more than a set of corrections or codes. It acts as a means of communication to both pupils and parents as to how the individual is performing, but is not an end in itself. Marking can encourage pupils to focus positively on errors. If pupils are encouraged to do something with the work after marking, for example redrafting or a further task based on a specific structure causing problems, then corrections become more worthwhile. Most importantly, marking should include some feedback to pupils in order to help them to improve their work. Even conscientious regular marking which only conveys a number on a page fails to provide the pupil with the kind of information which can help to improve performance. Constructive feedback and target setting can make a real difference in improving pupil performance and raising standards.

Marking

For marking to be effective it must be clearly understood by the pupils, it must be based on consistent standards and it must reflect agreed criteria. (Williams 1999: 13)

 10

Trainee/NQT Task

Marking – the big questions!

Consider your initial responses to the following items:

• Purpose of marking: why do we mark?

• Who should mark (pupil, peer, teacher, others)?

• What should be marked?

• How often and when should we mark?

• What criteria should be used and how?

There are no 'easy' answers to these questions, but it is important to keep them in mind as you read this chapter and develop your assessment practice.

This section contains general information and pointers on marking policy and practice:

- the purpose of marking;
- some general principles of marking;
- the kinds of systems used;
- ways of developing departmental policy.

So why mark? Firstly, it helps us to identify levels of attainment and check the effectiveness of our teaching. It acts as a means of providing students and parents with feedback on progress and performance. It is a useful tool to monitor individual needs and help identify special educational needs (including those of the most able). Finally, it helps motivate learners during their continuous learning process.

Marking, then, is not a purpose in itself. We need to consider carefully the nature of the task to ensure that it has a purpose to practise a particular structure or skill, that it is achievable yet challenging, and that it is of interest to pupils. Work marked should also cover all Attainment Targets, for example reading an article and summarising it, listening to a report and taking notes or recording oneself on cassette are all valid tasks.

When trainees are about to mark their first pieces of pupils' work, they typically ask questions such as:

- What does marking involve?
- What marks do we make on the page?
- How do we score the answers?
- What does the final mark represent/not represent?
- What happens as a result of the information recorded?

These questions are perfectly valid and are at the heart of what marking involves. These and others are considered in this chapter.

When marking pupils' work, you need to think about the following:

- The nature of the task – is it open-ended? For example, a task where a pupil can reach as far as possible. Is it closed? For example, only a particular AT level is possible.
- How directed were the instructions or how creative could the pupil be? Can you allocate marks for specific items?
- If using ICT, be clear how you're marking the language and/or the ICT: beware that the presentation may mask the quality of the language!
- What exactly is being marked – knowledge, understanding, creativity, effort, accuracy, fluency, etc?

  11

Trainee/NQT Task

How do you mark?

- Reflect on **how** to mark pupils' work. Think carefully about what you have seen in schools. What is most effective?
  - Use of the target language – comments in TL or in English?
  - Colour of ink/pencil.
  - Accuracy/spelling/corrections.
  - Use of marks or grades.
  - Departmental symbols/codes.
  - Positive marking.

- With your mentor, decide on a task you will assess. Identify how you will set, mark and give feedback to pupils. Evaluate how effective your assessment was: what did it tell you about your teaching, pupil learning, future planning?

Some marking principles, which are useful to bear in mind are to:

- make your marking clear, prompt and regular;
- use a system which is thorough, systematic and constructive;
- include marks/comments/feedback for both class work and homework;
- deal with common problems as a class;
- cover all four ATs;
- use meaningful comments (target language) to give informative feedback;
- check departmental policy;
- enter all marks into your mark book;
- return marked work to pupils in good time;
- remember that marking is essential for the pupil **and** the teacher.

It could be questioned whether we should award **marks** all the time. Marks could be viewed as a discouragement for weaker pupils.

An effective marking system should be consistently implemented, be easily understood by the pupils and be positive and encouraging about their work. An impression mark or comment is not particularly helpful, and returning work covered in red ink, grades or mysterious symbols without explanations can prove demotivating for pupils. Marking work is our way of providing feedback to pupils in order to help them to improve. Marking should not be discouraging to pupils but should be sensitive and constructive, and include some positive feedback to create a positive learning experience. Marking is a way of communicating with pupils and can have a real effect on confidence and enthusiasm, on how pupils perceive themselves and on their self-esteem. If progress and achievement are emphasised rather than failure, learner motivation is more likely to follow. It is helpful to make it clear to pupils what aspects of the work are being marked and, in order to open the door to further achievement and improvement, it is important to give them an achievable target **and** tell them how they can do it. The following ideas come from a school in Coventry.

Ideas for marking

1 Use a different colour pen from the colour the pupil has used.

2 Ensure neat handwriting (otherwise you can't expect it from them!).

3 Set targets when possible (in English?).

4 Use the school/departmental marking policy (helps students to follow one system).

5 Use TL where possible.

6 Allow time to go through work marked in class (often they make similar mistakes).

7 Show examples of incorrect work (without names) and ask students to analyse/correct it.

8 Discuss feedback individually (time permitting).

9 Adapt your style of marking according to the Key Stage.

10 Always try to be positive/encouraging (if they've tried hard anyway!)

Beware! Ensure you don't set huge amounts of work to mark that does not help learners and takes up a great deal of time to mark. Think carefully about what you are marking and why.

Organising marking – tips for PGCE trainees

Organising your time can sometimes be difficult! During your PGCE year you will need to:

1 plan every lesson;

2 make resources;

3 take part in extra-curricular activities;

4 mark 8 x 34 books every week!

Tips to help you organise the time you spend on marking:

- try to mark books every fortnight – it helps and saves a mountain of work getting on top of you;

- select five books per set and give detailed targets. It isn't always possible to give targets to every student every time!

- for vocabulary and spelling tests, get students to mark their own or a partner's from time to time;

- for oral work – get the class to judge their ability;

- tapes are a quick way to mark and give feedback;

- mark a draft but not a final piece of work – the latter should be perfect.

Source: Maria Cutler, Coundon Court School

Organising marking – tips for NQTs

Marking work is a good way of getting to know pupils and their level of ability. Quick marking as you go around in class is an important way of checking that pupils are on task and at the same time improving classroom management. It also provides immediate feedback to pupils, checks on pupils' learning and the effectiveness of your own teaching, as well as reducing the burden of marking later. Taking exercise books in every week at the start of the term and returning marked work promptly will set the right ground rules of expectations and show pupils you value the task and their performance. This then makes continuing with this schedule much more manageable and effective. Plan your schedule of marking to fit in with your timetable. Providing brief feedback with ways to improve work will encourage pupils to be fully involved in their learning from the start so that they are clear how they can progress. This involvement can be further developed by getting pupils to mark their own and others' work using simplified mark schemes (see also Appendix 3).

As a trainee or more experienced teacher in the MFL department, it is important to refer to the departmental marking policy when marking pupils' work. You will need to think carefully about how you set out your mark book, ensuring that you record marks for **all** Attainment Targets.

Departmental marking policy

The best departments seize the opportunity to shape pupils' expectations in MFL from the start of Key Stage 3. They have a rigorous but formative approach to routine marking and to the assessment of oral work during lessons and a focus on developing an accurate grasp of structure, and they make it clear why and how pupils need to improve. Assessment of oral work in lessons takes account of what pupils can do, and provides encouragement but not false praise. Such assessment takes place in a range of contexts including whole class question and answer work, pair work, pupil presentations, but always with clearly targeted outcomes, such as learning new structures or vocabulary. These assessments raise pupils' sights, for example using new idioms for the more able, while at the same time giving credit for 'being close' to a pupil who has not fully grasped a point, and guiding pupils to a fully correct response. (OFSTED 2002a)

Despite such good practice in some departments, other departments are still searching for effective marking and assessment systems, as exemplified by this comment by a Head of Department:

I am currently updating our departmental handbook and reviewing our marking policy. We need to find a simple, manageable marking system which ideally includes a way of rewarding effort as well as attainment so as not to demoralise our less able students.

The following departmental task would be a useful starting point in developing or refining a departmental policy on marking (see also Appendices 1 and 2). There is an additional departmental INSET activity in Chapter 7 (INSET/ITE Task 7, p135).

8

Departmental Task

Marking overview

Reflect on these questions:

- Homework/class work – are they marked differently?
- What forms of marking are appropriate for particular activities (see below)?
- Who is marking intended for?
- Who marks? Are there times when peer/self/group can mark? How could they be enabled to mark their own work?
- How often do you **a)** record marks **b)** take exercise books/other work in?
- What criteria are used when you mark? Would someone else mark the work and come up with the same result?
- How far should pupils be aware of the criteria by which work is being assessed?
- How do you ensure that all four Attainment Targets are 'marked'?
- What does the 'mark' communicate to the pupil/the teacher/the parent?
- What scope should pupils have for discussing their reactions to the marks received?
- Does anything follow on from the 'mark'? If so, what?
- When are comments more appropriate than marks (and possibly vice versa)?
- How could pupils be trained to think about redrafting or correcting their work?
- How would you mark a draft and then a redraft?
- How could information on NC level descriptions be made comprehensible and relevant to the pupils?
- How could the department build a common idea of what kind of performance constitutes a particular level or grade?
- How could the department build a common idea of what practical activities and/or resources provide good opportunities for this type of performance?

In the appendices you will find:

- two departmental policies (Appendix 1, p138 and Appendix 2, p140) – you could compare these with your own and agree any adaptations within your department;
- a mark scheme for KS3 (see Appendix 3, p141) which includes a range of correcting symbols and departmental advice on corrections.

 12

Trainee/NQT Task

Developing accurate judgements in marking pupils' work

Obtain some examples of marked and unmarked work from your department.

- Photocopy some unmarked work.
- Mark this work according to the departmental policy and note any issues that arise.
- Discuss the outcomes with your mentor or Head of Department.

Correcting work (oral and written)

Learner errors are a clear indication that learning is going on.
(Macaro 1997)

It is, of course, recognised that error-making is an integral part of the process of language learning. Even teachers, as so-called experts, make errors from time to time. Yet, as languages teachers, we need to make decisions in every lesson about whether learner errors should be corrected, which types should be corrected and how they should be corrected at various phases of the learning process. We often feel tempted to correct every error instantly as it occurs, whereas we need to consider the type of error, whether it interferes with communicating the message or whether it comes about as a result of pupils being more adventurous and creative with language. Clearly, if pupils make an error while practising a teaching point, this should be corrected sensitively straight away, perhaps by involving the whole class in further repetition of the correct form or pronunciation, or by repeating the sentence containing the error highlighting (by stress) the correct version. Other ways of correcting errors might include:

- asking the pupil to repeat what he or she said;
- showing by a gesture that an error has been made to encourage self-correction;
- pointing out the error and asking the pupil him- or herself to correct the error;
- asking another pupil to correct the error;
- explaining why something is wrong;
- remodelling the sentence.

When pupils are involved in more open-ended tasks, it is often better to wait until the end of the activity/presentation/performance to correct a selection of pervasive and systematic errors (where pupils have consistent difficulty with a particular aspect of pronunciation, grammar or lexis). Pupils will benefit from concrete examples of errors. For example, general comments like 'you need to work on your past tense' could be more helpful if specific instances are pointed out with the correct version. Errors often simply signal the need for further practice.

Reflection Task

What do pupils think?

Think about a group of pupils you know well.

- What do you think their feelings and attitudes toward error correction are?
- What error correction strategies would be most effective for them?

Going over a test or piece of work

The benefits of completing corrections are undoubted if work is marked promptly and corrections are done as work is returned in class time. In other words, to make correction (especially delayed correction) worthwhile, it is important to make sure pupils **do something with it,** e.g. redrafting the work, completing a task based on corrections, or saying why something is wrong. Going over a test or piece of work and working through any errors needs to be handled carefully, for example:

- go over the work on an OHT, perhaps with an overlay of the correct responses;
- discuss the work and show possible responses, perhaps even before they get their own tests back, so their attention is fully on the work;
- after giving back a test, put up the correct answers and get pupils to add corrections in a different colour pen;
- collect examples of (anonymous) common mistakes from a homework exercise and go through them on the board with the whole class, then ask pupils to say what is wrong with the examples;
- mark homework (e.g. as long a description of a town as pupils could write) without correcting it, then underline errors and add omission marks and hand back to pupils and get them to work in pairs with a dictionary to try to improve the level of each piece of work.

Error correction

The following is an excerpt from Tile Hill Wood School and Language College departmental policy on marking in modern languages.

> Generally, every error is marked, although this may depend on the student's ability and the focus of the work, particularly in the case of Special Needs pupils. Date, title, headings are always written in the target language and checked for accuracy. Mistakes are corrected in full the first time they occur and subsequently underlined. It is best to write out the whole word containing the mistake either above the error or in the margin.
>
> *Source: Tile Hill Wood School and Language College*

Marking can be used to highlight errors which are to be avoided, but can also be used positively to highlight desirable content. For example, when marking, highlight the 'good' bits so that pupils know the kind of elements which will raise their (NC) level. Equally, highlight the 'bad' bits in a different colour to show pupils what should never be seen. In this way raised expectations can push for the highest level possible. In order to raise achievement, it is helpful to make pupils aware of what they need to do to reach the next level, e.g. to reach Level 5: include present tense + past tense or future tense; opinions (descriptions, including comparisons).

The following examples of comments come again from Tile Hill Wood School.

> **Expecting pupils to learn from corrections**
> (Devote time to this as a matter of course when books are returned).
>
> - *Corrige, s'il te plaît/A corriger!*
> - Can you correct this verb/adjective, etc and show me?
> - How do you make an adjective agree in Fr/Sp?
> - Write out a fair copy please.
> - Correct your mistakes carefully by ...
> - Just two verb endings/adjective agreements/genders, etc to check.
> - Ask me if you're not sure about ...
>
> *Source: Tile Hill Wood School and Language College*

Electronic marking

Some language-specific software and interactive CD-ROMs provide instant, automatic feedback for the learner. In this case teachers need to check the appropriateness of such feedback and help pupils interpret it. A module on computer-aided assessment (CAA) and language learning can be accessed at **www.ict4lt.org**.

Pupils can also word process assignments and submit them to their teacher electronically (via the Web, e-mail or over a local network). The teacher can mark the work electronically without printing it by using tools present in word-processing packages (e.g. using the **Insert Comment** function). Corrections and comments can be added and the work returned to the pupil electronically. Pupils can then easily re-draft their work using the teacher's comments. Examples of how this can be done also appear on the **ict4lt** website mentioned above.

Expectations of trainees during school placements

Higher education institutions and their partnership schools will naturally devise their own expectations of trainees' contribution to assessment during school placements. This is one example devised by MFL tutors at the University of Warwick and mentors in partnership schools:

M I N I M U M   A S S E S S M E N T   E X P E C T A T I O N S

The following are our **minimum** expectations of you during school placements:

- that you will collect in and mark **all** pupils' work **at least** once a fortnight;

- that you will record all marks appropriately for each pupil;

- that you will provide constructive feedback to all pupils;

- that you will evaluate the teaching and learning in all your lessons and series of lessons;

- that you will record a range of marks across all Attainment Targets for all classes;

- that you will use the information thus gained in your future planning;

- that you will investigate a range of assessment strategies.

These minimum assessment expectations could be used in conjunction with Departmental Task 3 on p48.

A case study follows to illustrate the marking process. The teacher provides the background to the task, along with an example of a pupil's response and what she learnt from it as a teacher.

Marking case study

This is the work of a top set of three (Year 9) in a Foundation Secondary School. The work is an example of writing independently following a series of lessons about TV and cinema.

The brief had been to write about three TV programmes, two that pupils liked and one they didn't, giving reasons and opinions. For cinema, the brief was to write about films they had seen.

It was very important that I marked the books after this. Some pupils had completed everything and as you can see, written to a high standard. Yes, there were errors but the pupils were pushing the boundaries of the French they know. Unfortunately, at the other end of the scale, were those who had done the minimum, almost nothing really and some books were missing.

All pupils were working at least at Level 5, with knowledge of present and past tenses.

I intended to give everyone the chance to complete this work to the highest standard possible for each individual.

Why was it important to look at the books?

I could see how well (or not) the group understood the work. It was time for me to step in and go over, explain again points of structure and grammar which some pupils desperately needed if they were to be able to write independently.

The next lesson will go like this:

1 Oral revision of basic vocab with film and TV.

2 Return exercise books and explain clearly to the class just what has been marked and what I was looking for.

3 *Le corrigé:* everyone now writes this title and as I go over the errors they will make notes.

4 Date now and title *L'écrit: notre but.*

(This is to remind the pupils what we are about)

Aim: to write independently, accurately and in an interesting manner. To discover language for myself from dictionaries and from lessons: texts both listening and reading and from vocabulary.

5 OHP: on which I have typed these good examples from both boys and girls and not the obvious pupils all the time.

This fulfils several issues. It can remind the class of points of grammar, the weaker ones can get further ideas and the good ones can feel pleased to see their work there.

6 Foreign Language Assistant: she will work in small oral room with a chosen group who have all done well and completed all the work to a good standard. Nine pupils, a tenth to join if he finishes.

- They will read out aloud their work.
- They will interview each other
- They will read more complex accounts about films.

7 The rest will redraft or complete their work, aiming to fulfil the aim of the lesson.

I have included an example of the highest level of work here, and had a further two examples to provide moderation material.

Matthew (work included below): everything already completed. Excellent work, pushing the limits of his French.

Simon (work not reproduced here): everything completed. He tries very hard but he needs more time to think about how to construct accurate sentences.

Ross (work not reproduced here): incomplete work. Has written about TV but nothing about films and little in the way of his report from the interview. He needs time to complete all of this.

Ce que j'aime (ou pas) regarder

J'aime regarder 'The Simpsons'. Ça passe à la télé cinq fois par semaine, le lundi, mardi, mercredi, jeudi et vendredi. Il s'agit d'une famille rigolo et amusant. Quelquefois, c'est un peu violent. Il passe à six heures et c'est un dessin animé.

J'ai regardé 'The Nutty Professor', c'est un film comique. C'est tellement rigolo, un film qui me fait rire. Je l'ai en vidéo et je le regarde souvent. Eddie Murphy et Janet Jackson sont les vedettes et Eddie Murphy joue tous les membres de la famille Klump.

Il s'agit d'une famille disfonctionelle. C'est un dessin animé et une comédie.

J'aime regarder 'Wild'. Ca passe à la télé une fois par semaine le dimanche à sept heures le soir. C'est un documentaire d'animal et c'est tellement éducatif.

Je n'aime pas regarder 'Eastenders' parce que c'est en mauvais goût, ennuyeux et il y a des histoires mal conçues. Ça passe quatre fois à huit heures du soir. C'est éducatif pour comment se comporter mal.

Source: Studley High School

Giving feedback

Assessment is not only concerned with academic output, whether in listening, reading, speaking or writing. Successful feedback concentrates on those areas which will help a learner identify issues and improve their understanding and performance. This includes inevitably learning strategies, attitudes, self-esteem, making connections. Broadfoot (2000: 212) explains it as follows:

> *Existing approaches to assessment are almost exclusively concerned with explicit learning, with measuring what has been consciously learned and reproduced in a formal setting. However the goals of learning are likely in the future to centre increasingly on the acquisition of attitudes, skills and personal qualities, since the acquisition of knowledge, formerly the core of the curriculum, is likely to become more and more irrelevant by its universal availability at the push of a button. It is the ability to know what knowledge is needed, to know how to look for it and be able to apply it, that is likely to become central.*

Although assessment and testing are sometimes perceived negatively by pupils and teachers alike, it is precisely this process which can be extremely effective in helping pupils to make progress and to know how to improve.

A recent study (Wiliam and Black 2002) showed that pupils' national test and GCSE results improved by more than half a grade when teachers stopped giving marks out of 10, made greater use of their day-to-day assessment of pupils and gave them detailed feedback. Their findings suggest that tests and targets do not in themselves raise standards and that quality feedback from teachers is crucial. This feedback needs to be acted upon by pupils to involve them in their own learning.

Feedback of progress and performance is vital for every learner. Feedback may take a variety of forms: to a whole class (perhaps picking up on common errors and practising the correct version as a group), face-to-face to an individual or, in a written form at the end of a piece of work or recorded on tape for recorded speaking tasks. Information gained from assessment needs to be communicated constructively to learners in order to give useful advice, to encourage them to reflect upon and evaluate their work and achievement. When teachers assess learner performance in any of the skills, they are determining gaps in learning, and to qualify as feedback, the information given must be useful in closing the gap between the actual and the desired levels of performance. The teacher needs to be clear what constitutes mistakes in the strictest meaning of the term or unacceptable deviations from the expected norm and feed back to the learner some element of prescription about what must be done to remedy mistakes or improve performance.

What could feedback include?

Feedback could include:

- encouragement in the form of praise while providing a clear identification of good points, (for example, 'good use of past tenses', 'excellent range of expressions of time', etc);
- rewards (points for oral contribution; raffle tickets for oral contributions/ good effort/good work drawn at the end of the week/half term/term; merits, commendations, etc according to the school system; 'Person of the lesson', etc;

Responding to pupils' work effectively

- identification of mistakes and errors through a code system of marks and symbols familiar to the pupil;
- points which require more work on the part of the pupil, (for example, 'copy spellings carefully', 'can you give an example sentence for where you would use *que* and another for *qui* please?');
- some detail about how the work could be improved, (for example, 'include more opinions', 'a range of different subjects');
- linguistic advice (for example, notes on grammar points);
- what further strategies the pupil could employ (for example, ideas for learning vocabulary).

Too much criticism can be undermining, while positive, supportive feedback with constructive messages about concrete ways to improve can be encouraging and motivating and can be a factor in increasing confidence.

The pupil work below shows a piece of marked work with explicit feedback: a Year 7 task and one pupil's response, with accompanying marks and feedback.

The Task as Set to the Pupils

[Attainment Target 4; National Curriculum Level 3-4; Programme of Study 5f]

Name: _____

DIE ZIMMER - ROOMS

Mein Haus hat 9 Zimmer.	My house has 9 rooms.
In meinem Haus gibt es...	In my house there is ...
... ein Wohnzimmer	... a living-room
ein Schlafzimmer	a bedroom
ein Badezimmer	a bathroom
ein Esszimmer	a dining-room
ein Arbeitszimmer	a study
eine Küche	a kitchen
eineToilette	a toilet
einen Flur	a hall
einen Keller	a cellar
Es gibt ...	There is ...
... einen Garten	... a garden

Hausaufgaben

Title: 'Mein Traumhaus'

On A4 paper, draw, label (in German) and colour a plan of your dream house. Write a short paragraph underneath the plan, saying what sort of house it is and which rooms there are in it. Use this sheet to help you.   Hand in on Thursday!

Source: Elly Crofton, Coundon Court School

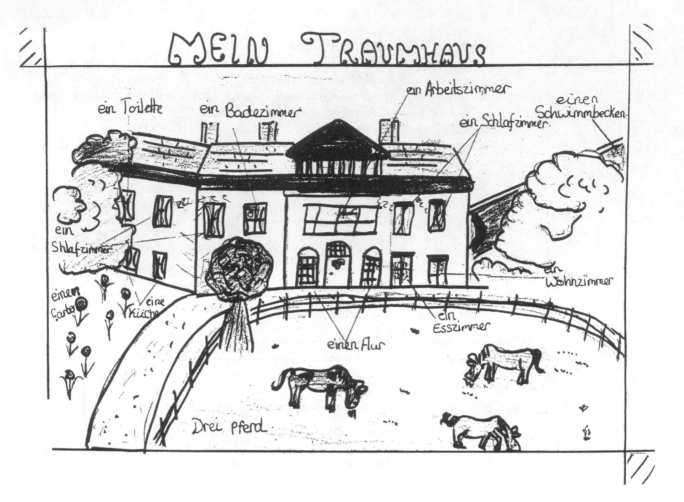

Mein Traumhaus ist sehr sehr groß und
alt. In meinem Haus gibt es ein Wohnzimmer,
achtzehn Shlafzimmers (You can only see 4)
fünf Badezimmers (You can only see 1) ein großes
Esszimmer, ein sehr großes Arbeitszimmer, eine
dopple Küche, eine Toilette, einen dopple Flur. Es
gibt einen Garten und drei Pferd!
Es gibt auch einen Schwimmbecken.

Creativity 10/10   Wunderbar Imogen!
Accuracy 9/10   You use the correct genders
NC Level 4b   and have included lots of detail.

★ 2 CREDITS.   Plural of 'Zimmer' is 'Zimmer' (no 's').
                               To increase your level further,
                               include an opinion too.

Source: Elly Crofton, Coundon Court School

Praise

It is important to include praise in feedback. The following examples come from Tile Hill Wood School and Language College marking policy:

- Stars > commendations.
- Target language expressions: *bravo ... super ... prima ... estupendo.*
- Commendations for 3 x ☺.
- Department speaking stickers.
- Comment on what has been done well, e.g. lots of time expressions used, good variety of subjects/opinions/range of vocabulary.
- I noticed you worked really well in today's lesson/in the role play activity/in the listening exercise, etc.
- I've really enjoyed ... *Ça me plaît beaucoup/ça m'a fait grand plaisir de lire!*
- You've worked really hard on this/you've put a lot of effort into this.
- Great, you've followed my advice, well done!

- I can see you've spent a lot of time on this.
- Well done for achieving your target.
- Good use of *pero/mais.*
- I particularly like the questions you have included/your final comment/your use of ...
- Excellent – lots of accurate French – particularly your use of adjectives – and your ending is perfect. Well done!
- This is very promising – keep up the good work!
- I'm very pleased with the details in your answers.
- I'm pleased you have incorporated some of the vocabulary the assistant used.
- Excellent predictions before we listened to the tape.

Source: Tile Hill Wood School and Language College

Oral feedback

The following transcript provides an example of oral feedback.

Example of teacher's feedback transcribed from the comments recorded at the end of a pupil's recorded speaking task

Pupils' task: to describe family

Merci beaucoup, (name of pupil). *Un bon travail. Bonne grammaire.* A few things to look through on the pronunciation. You said the word 'fifty' – it's *'cinquante',* pronounce the *'t'* on the end, not *'cinquan(te)'.* The word for bald is *'chauve'.* You said your dad was generous – *'généreux'* and your mum's hardworking *'travailleuse'* (pronunciation corrected). Check on how you said those: *'généreux'* and *'travailleuse'.* And then the main problem seemed to be when you were using some of the joining words to make more complex sentences: when you said because 'he is' or 'because she is',

it's *'parce qu'il est'* or *'parce qu'elle est',* not (attempt at mispronunciation) – oh, I'm not sure what you said actually, but it's *'parce qu'il est'* or *'parce qu'elle est'.* You were saying what I like about or what I don't like about somebody in my family it's *'c'est qu'elle est'.* OK? You've got the *qu* then the apostrophe and either *elle* or *il* so it sort of runs into one word: *'c'est qu'elle est', 'c'est qu'il est',* alright? And I think it was your sister who is younger than you *'elle est plus jeune que moi'* I think you said *'plus jeune qui moi'* which makes it 'younger **who** me' rather than 'younger **than** me'. *Alors, note sur vingt, je te donne dix-sept, oui, dix-sept sur vingt. Merci.*

Source: Maria Cutler, Coundon Court School

Developmental feedback

Many departments now issue pupils with their own copies of the assessment criteria and/or the mark scheme. If the criteria are detailed enough, this too will give pupils clear guidelines about the kind of learning in which they need to engage next, where effort should be concentrated (vocabulary/tenses/skills) and where specific improvements can be made to reach a higher level of performance. Pupil-friendly level descriptions (see Appendix 5, p146) or descriptions of different grade definitions (see p97) are helpful in making explicit to pupils what is expected at each level or grade. Equally, pupils need to be clear about what constitutes good performance in each element of the course. Models of what is expected at a given standard which pupils can imitate and adapt are helpful in communicating to pupils exactly what is required at a particular level or stage.

Listening and reading tasks are often viewed merely as **testing** comprehension where the answer is simply right or wrong. However, all skills in foreign language learning are progressive and developmental, and feedback on listening and reading comprehensions can be used to help the pupils acquire further learning or coping strategies. For example, transcripts can be used to emphasise aspects of aural discrimination and develop familiarity with difficult sounds in the target language. Pupils also need to develop the skill of listening for gist and recognising marker words, for example, and become sensitive to interpreting what they actually hear. It is not much help simply to be told the right answer.

Collating responses

When collating answers from an activity (which could be listening, speaking, reading, writing or a mixture), it is often appropriate to provide written back-up for answers given by pupils, e.g. write them on the board, or fill in the OHT appropriately. How will you find out how well they did/what they didn't understand?

- Take general feedback?
- Ask for who got 6? 7? 8? 9? 10?
- Exploit certain bits further, e.g. for cultural awareness?
- Take more than one person's suggestion for what is the correct answer?
- Will you record the marks by pupils telling you their scores for you to write down, or take the papers/books in or not record the marks at all?

Reflection Task

Target language comments

Look at the bullet point list below. What target language comments could you use to fulfil each one?

> **Feedback during and after lessons**
>
> Feedback on content (adapted from Richards and Lockhart, 1994: 189):
>
> - acknowledging a correct answer;
> - indicating an incorrect answer;
> - praising;
> - expanding or modifying a student's answer;
> - repeating;
> - summarising;
> - criticising.

9

Reflection Task

Look at the bullet point list below. When do you think the different ways of providing feedback on form would be appropriate and when not?

Feedback on form (adapted from Richards and Lockhart, 1994: 190):

- asking the student to repeat what he or she said;
- pointing out the error and asking the student to self-correct;
- commenting on an error and explaining why it is wrong, without having the student repeat the correct form;
- asking another student to correct the error;
- using a gesture to indicate that an error has been made.

In Years 7–9 the emphasis in the first instance is on good presentation and accurate copying of new words and phrases. A numerical mark may be appropriate for reading/listening exercises and vocabulary tests which are stuck in at the back of books. Positive comments which recognise the student's effort and personal progress are used. **Specific advice for improvement** should be given where possible. This is often appropriate with the end of unit activities, e.g. video, poem, survey, display work, postcard, etc. This is formative for the student, useful for our forward planning and helps familiarise students with our expectations of them. Advice may be given in the target language or English.

Source: Tile Hill Wood School and Language College

The following pages provide examples of detailed feedback which the MFL department at Ashlawn Bilateral School has developed for each year group for specific assessment points. The two examples here communicate a level of performance with justifications, as well as targets indicating ways a pupil can improve.

Year 11 French Gold Star Marking Feedback
Extended Writing on Holidays

Name..................................... Teacher.......................Date..............

You are currently working at around a grade _____

This is because:

- ☐ You communicate occasional words only.
- ☐ You communicate simple facts.
- ☐ You communicate simple facts and some details (eg opinions).
- ☐ You give a lot of information, including opinions, descriptions and accounts.
- ☐ You give lots of information, narrate events, give full descriptions, and express and justify ideas and points of view.

- ☐ Your writing includes occasional words that can be recognised.
- ☐ You use simple vocabulary and structures and short sentences.
- ☐ You use appropriate words and structures, but they are simple.
- ☐ You link appropriate words and fairly varied structures together with joining words.
- ☐ You vary vocabulary, use a variety of structures, longer sentences, more than one tense and express opinions well.
- ☐ You describe and give opinions with a wide range of words and structures, use long sentences and subordinate clauses successfully and regularly.
- ☐ You use a very wide range of appropriate words and structures effectively. You write long, complex sentences well, and the piece of writing is fluent and confident.

- ☐ Structures are not really understood.
- ☐ Basic structures contain major mistakes and are often incorrectly used.
- ☐ Most sentences contain mistakes, some major, and verbs are often wrongly constructed.
- ☐ There are some major errors and many minor ones. Many verbs are not correct.
- ☐ There are many minor errors and a few big ones, including verbs, but the writing is easy to understand.
- ☐ Errors are minor, major ones occasionally occur in complex sentences. Most verbs are correctly formed.
- There are hardly any errors. The piece is accurate and verbs are correctly formed.

You now need to work towards reaching a grade _____ in your writing.
You can do this by:

- ☐ Communicating simple facts.
- ☐ Communicating simple facts and some details (eg opinions).
- ☐ Giving a lot of information, including opinions, descriptions and accounts.
- ☐ Giving lots of information, narrating events, giving full descriptions, and expressing and justifying ideas and points of view.

- ☐ Writing with simple vocabulary and structures and short sentences.
- ☐ Using appropriate simple words and structures well.
- ☐ Linking appropriate words and fairly varied structures together with joining words.
- ☐ Varying vocabulary, using a variety of structures, longer sentences, more than one tense and expressing opinions well.
- ☐ Describing and giving opinions with a wide range of words and structures, using long sentences and subordinate clauses successfully and regularly.

☐	Using a very wide range of appropriate words and structures effectively, writing long, complex sentences well, and ensuring the piece of writing is fluent and confident.

☐	Writing basic structures with only minor mistakes.
☐	Writing basic structures with only minor errors, and forming most verbs correctly.
☐	Writing a variety of structures with only minor errors, and forming most verbs correctly.
☐	Making few errors, most minor, and producing work that is easy to understand.
☐	Forming verbs and most structures correctly, with only a few errors in complex structures.
☐	Writing highly accurate French, including complex structures and verb formation.

☐	Including the past tense (what you did).
☐	Including a variety of past tense (with etre/ avoir, je/nous/il/ils..).
☐	Including the present tense (what you normally do) .
☐	Including a variety of present tense (-er/re/ir verbs, irregular, je/nous/il/ils..)
☐	Including the future tense (what you will do).
☐	Including a variety of future tense (with je vais and –ai ending in je form, je/nous/il/ils..)
☐	Including the imperfect tense (what you were doing).
☐	Describing what people and places are/were like.
☐	Describing what happened in detail.
☐	Using paragraphs and structuring your work.
☐	Including an introduction and a conclusion.
☐	Using an infinitive as a second verb and after a/ de/ pour/ etc.
☐	Using an apostrophe for je m'appelle, nous n'allons pas, etc.
☐	Including a variety of opinions.
☐	Justifying opinions with complex viewpoints.
☐	Checking that you have included accents.
☐	Agreeing adjectives with e/s/es/ etc.
☐	Checking whether words are masculine (le/un/du/etc) or feminine (la/une/de la / etc).
☐	Other:

Student response:

Source: Ashlawn Bilateral School

Year 8 Sports et Loisirs Assessment Gold Star Feedback

Name.................................... Teacher......................Date..............

- ☐ You understand a range of familiar statements, with repetition.
- ☐ You understand short familiar written phrases.
- ☐ You write short phrases with several errors.
- ☐ You understand short passages of familiar language and identify main points, likes and dislikes, at normal speed, with some repetition.
- ☐ You understand short texts/ dialogues and note main points and opinions.
- ☐ You write short phrases from memory, to make up a short paragraph, with few errors.
- ☐ You understand simple sentences in longer passages, noting main points and details, with some repetition.
- ☐ You understand texts, and note main points and details.
- ☐ You write sentences, with few errors, opinions and details, in a paragraph.
- ☐ You understand spoken language from several topics, including present and past or future events, noting main points, details and opinions.
- ☐ You understand a range of written material, including present and past or future events, noting main points, details and opinions.
- ☐ You use two tenses to convey information and opinions, and although there may be errors in forming verbs, it is easy to understand what you mean.

National curriculum level=	Listening	Reading	Writing	Average
% in test =	☐	☐	☐	☐

Other comments on achievement:

On the next page are targets which you need to work towards to reach a level ☐
Write three which you will work on straight away here:

☐ You understand a range of familiar statements, with repetition.

☐ You understand short familiar written phrases.

☐ You write short phrases with several errors.

☐ You understand short spoken passages of familiar language and identify main points, likes and dislikes, at normal speed, with some repetition.

☐ You understand short texts/ dialogues and note main points and opinions.

☐ You write short phrases from memory, to make up a short paragraph, with few errors.

☐ You understand simple spoken sentences in longer passages, noting main points and details, with some repetition.

☐ You understand texts, and note main points and details.

☐ You write sentences, with few errors, opinions and details, in a paragraph.

☐ You understand spoken language from several topics, including present and past or future events, noting main points, details and opinions.

☐ You understand a range of written material, including present and past or future events, noting main points, details and opinions.

☐ You use two tenses to convey information and opinions, and although there may be errors in forming verbs, it is easy to understand what you mean.

☐ You understand short taped narratives, covering all three tenses and including unfamiliar contexts, interference and hesitancy, and note main points, specific details and points of view, with little repetition.

☐ You understand short written narratives, covering all three tenses and including unfamiliar contexts, interference and hesitancy, and note main points, specific details and points of view, with little repetition.

☐ You write confidently and accurately in three tenses/ timeframes, while using varied language and structures.

☐ You use your exercise book and worksheets for revision.

☐ You structure work in paragraphs in a sensible order.

☐ You check all your spellings carefully.

☐ You put é on past tense verb endings, eg j'ai aimé

☐ You put accents on your work.

☐ Other:

Source: Ashlawn Bilateral School

Ideas for developing the effectiveness of your marking

The following material looks at ways to develop the effectiveness of your marking.

Reference to NC levels

✔ Note what is required for the forthcoming test, e.g. writing frame ... main contents ... technique.

✔ Specific feedback on test results, tips for success next time.

✔ Student involvement in target setting: transfer targets from review/reports into back of exercise books.

• Almost a level ... What do you have to do now in order to improve?

• You've achieved level ... because ...

• You need to incorporate link words, opinions and reference to either the past or the future for Level 5.

• Can you add a couple of verbs in the past tense to move up to Level 6?

• Now try to use the future/past tense accurately by yourself in your next piece of writing to get Level 6.

• To make your Level 5/6 more secure aim to include several verbs in the past/future tenses.

• You have understood the gist, now try to listen out for more details to get a higher level in your listening.

• Use grids for speaking assessments showing tasks completed, any errors, comments on pronunciation, level achieved and targets.

• Accents are important!

• Avoid repeating yourself: try to vary the phrases you use.

• I think this would benefit from more careful planning – can you organise your ideas into paragraphs?

• How could you join these two short sentences?

• Could you give a reason for your opinion?

• Read through your writing before handing it in – I'm sure you could have spotted some of these mistakes and have corrected them for yourself.

• Base what you write on the model/the work we do in class.

• Refer to your notes on ...

• How much of this can you memorise?

• Get ... to have a look at this and take a look at hers. How have you done this work differently?

• Work on sounding French/Spanish/German.

• Use the techniques we've talked about, i.e. skimming, scanning ...

• Now review your targets.

Extension ideas

• Read ... article in ... magazine in the library.

• Find out what the assistant thinks about this.

• Could you include some vocabulary from previous topics?

• How could you make this more interesting?

• Could you add some extra detail?

• Try to vary the subject, e.g. describe what 'we' do/your friend does/likes etc.

• Have a look at ... website.

• Look at your levels sheet to see what you need to do to move on to the next level.

• Rewrite using these link words.

How to achieve a personal approach/dialogue

• Ask individuals specific questions or make individual comments which require a response (comment on something which happened in lesson or something you know they are interested in). First task for pupils when books are returned.

• Half-termly comment on work and behaviour in general.

• I've noticed that you have been trying really hard with ... lately. Keep it up!

• The work you did on ... was great. *Bravo!*

• *Moi aussi! Je suis d'accord! Je ne suis pas de ton avis!*

• *Et toi, ... quelle est ta matière préférée? Quelle était la matière préférée de ta mère?*

• *Qu'est-ce que tu penses de ...?*

Source: Tile Hill Wood School and Language College

To sum up, effective feedback should have all of the following characteristics. It should be:

- ongoing – given throughout the learner's development;
- positive – informing the learner of what has been achieved;
- appropriate to the level/standard/stage at which the learner is operating;
- specific – relating to particular targets so that learners know where they are performing well and where further development needs to take place;
- constructive – if the learner is not doing something well, any barriers to progress should be identified and suggestions made about how to improve performance.

> *Feedback needs to be an interactive process that motivates and encourages pupils to take responsibility for their own learning, to evaluate their own progress and to be able to progress to higher levels.* (Hunt, 2001: 175)

Target setting

> *Targets = prediction plus challenge.* (Brooks 2002: 149)

The Inclusion statement in the National Curriculum also states that teachers should take specific action to respond to pupils' diverse needs by setting targets for learning.

> *Teachers should set targets for learning that:*
> - *build on pupils' knowledge, experiences, interests and strengths to improve areas of weakness and demonstrate progression over time*
> - *are attainable and yet challenging and help pupils to develop their self-esteem and confidence in their ability to learn.*
>
> (National Curriculum: Modern Foreign Languages, 1999: 23)

In this climate of target setting, there is a clear need to encourage pupils to improve their performance in modern languages by setting regular targets. This entails gathering good quality assessment data and reviewing all the evidence of pupils' past achievements at the start of the year, establishing the baseline achievement for each key stage and setting sensible but challenging targets for the end of the year from the baseline in order to realise each individual's potential. Target setting should be a process which inspires and stimulates the best in both teachers and pupils. At the start of the year, an assessment carried out once you know the pupils will confirm whether targets are realistic; if there is a discrepancy, this could be discussed with senior management. Under-achievers need to be identified throughout the year and action plans put in place to help them back on course.

In order to achieve an overall target of a level or a grade, pupils need regular feedback on performance and targets of **what** and **how** to improve. These targets need to be monitored and reviewed on a regular basis and might include oral feedback, written comments on class or homework or more formal targets written on a report for parents and pupils. Target setting can be linked with formative assessment. Learners benefit from knowing what to expect and what is expected of them. Once a piece of work has been marked, pupils can receive feedback on the work and targets of how they might improve it. This could include linguistic, learning and behavioural targets: pupils need to know how they can improve and subsequently check whether they have achieved their targets. Targets, therefore, need to be specific with a clear purpose for pupils: 'learn vocabulary' or 'revise tenses' or 'check your grammar' are not enough. For example, general targets of improved contribution or concentration in class need to be accompanied by some specific way of achieving it:

Target	*Action to be taken*
• *contribute more in class*	• *aim to answer at least three questions every lesson*
• *improve concentration in class*	• *always sit at the front of the class where you can see clearly*

('Motivating learners at KS4', Andy Hodgkinson, Language World 2000)

 10

Reflection Task

Making general targets specific

Using the examples above, decide how you could make the general targets 'learn vocabulary' or 'revise tenses' or 'check your grammar' more specific.

Short-term targets

In a TES MFL Curriculum Special (Spring 2000), Peter Downes and Iain Mitchell commented that an MFL Department needs to look at the Verbal Reasoning Quotient (VRQ) scores or Cognitive Ability Test (CAT) scores when working out targets. For individual pupils, they continue, it is specific goals which matter. They argue that posters displaying how to achieve each level can help here, by conscious application of criteria. They state that target setting works '... because it helps pupils to focus on bite-size chunks of language and think, yes **think**, about what they are learning and why.' They give examples of specific, short-term targets which could help boys in particular:

■ fifteen more words this week;
■ two examples of the past tense;
■ four sentences with a subordinate clause;
■ 35 seconds of oral work without stopping.

Linked in with targets are models and benchmarks where learners have an idea of what they can strive towards. Coaches of excellent athletes do not only inform them where they are going wrong. They observe other top performers in action, and learn how to emulate. If you set a task for your pupils, particularly if it is a more open-ended one, work out how you can provide a model for them to work from.

We have included a Departmental Task on target setting in Chapter 7 (see p136).

 *Use different coloured pens for marking, feedback comment and target. It makes the distinction clear between each and pupils like the colours!* (PGCE trainee)

Target setting and getting!

The following looks at target setting and target getting from the perspective of a Head of Department.

The Head of Department's perspective

As a department we aim to have a consistent approach to assessment and to use our assessment to inform our teaching and to increase our students' attainment. Target setting is built into the overall programme of language learning from the start. Learning aims are fixed and shared with all pupils, so that it is clear to pupils what they need to do to succeed. KS2 and KS3 SATs scores in Maths, English and Science and other data such as reading age scores are noted from the school database in our mark books and used as an indicator of potential achievement at GCSE. At all stages pupils are encouraged to be aware of their own learning, to understand what is required at each point and to set targets for future learning. Formative assessment of day-to-day progress depends on prompt and regular marking of written work and written academic guidance explaining ways to improve to the student is provided twice per half term. We recognise and reward good effort and work wherever possible by using a selection of phrases for praise. Supported by the seconds in department, I am responsible for monitoring the marking of the department and we look at a sample of exercise books each term.

At KS3 pupils receive a sheet showing progress through the levels, indicating what a Year 7/8/9 Modern Languages pupil can do at each level and in each skill (see Appendix 5). There are implications for schemes of work if we are to coach the majority of our students to reach the expectations; we must ensure they are given the opportunity to work at these higher levels for long enough. Bearing in mind the capabilities of our groups, it is important to ensure early coverage of the tenses and then to recycle them in subsequent topics. As always we must share the level descriptors and assessment criteria with our students before they complete tasks. Early familiarisation with the grade descriptors and marking criteria is essential so that students know what they are aiming for. Students are made totally familiar with exam requirements at GCSE and are given grade descriptors for each skill outlining the kind of work which results in A, C, and F grades in pupil speak and examples of work at each grade. Student progress is monitored by the class teacher, the head of department and by the head teacher through Years 10 and 11 and, in particular, just before and after the mock examinations.

After the mock exam pupils receive exam marks and written feedback. Again they reflect on their performance and write out an evaluation including details of what they did to revise, their strong and weak points, a list of targets and a target grade with comments on how to achieve it. As Head of Department I visit all Year 11 classes to lead a discussion 'What will make the difference?' which encompasses attitude and revision techniques leading up to the exams. Each pupil has to reflect on the question: What will make the difference for you? Every pupil then chooses two strategies from the list of examples and writes them down. 'Expectations of our Year 11 students' (see p82 and Web template 6) which highlights the partnership between staff and students and a tick list of extra tasks to encourage independent work (see p85) are issued. It is hoped these processes will help to foster independent learning and a sense of personal responsibility. The Head Teacher talks to every pupil twice a year. The Head of Department and the Head Teacher see all underachieving borderline pupils. A full revision programme is encouraged before mocks and progress is checked before exams.

To develop independent learning teachers maintain a class folder including reports and pupil reviews. Pupils reflect on their learning by completing a Modern Languages Review (see p87). This includes reflection on aspects enjoyed the most, aspects found most difficult, how work has improved and three specific targets of how marks could be improved further. Reports to parents include comments on progress with specific targets for development. During the build-up to the GCSE exams pupils can refer to an extra task tick list of 'Tips for Success' including tips for exam preparation on the intranet and record what they do in preparation for the exam. Learning strategies are developed with students and referred to in class and emphasis is placed on developing technique in the different skills. Time to reflect on learning is built into lessons on a regular basis and pupils make a record of this in the form of a learning log (see example p85).

Source: Tile Hill Wood School and Language College

9

Departmental Task

┌───┐
Expectations of pupils

- Look at the example below of expectations from a Year 11 pupil.

- Adapt this example to create your own departmental benchmarks (this text is also available on the associated website, Web template 6).

- Give out sheets with these on to all Year 11 pupils, and/or enlarge them to display in classrooms.
└───┘

Web template **6**   **Expectations of pupils**

Expectations of pupils

This is what we expect from you:

- Full concentration and effort in class.

- Maximum use of lesson time with a punctual start and quick changeover of activities.

- A willingness to take part in class speaking activities. Remember – you need to practise for your individual oral which is worth 25% of the marks.

- Homework and coursework completed to the best of your ability and handed in on time.

- Vocabulary learning a little and often (use your revision guide and the strategies discussed in class).

- Be familiar with what is required for an A–C grade by referring to your grade descriptor and go for it!

Some extra effort on your part:

- Go the Open Language Centre before school/on Wednesday lunchtime to work on the 'Essentials, expressions or connections' software

- Revise topics already covered.

- Make sure you can use the past/present/future tense.

- Watch *GCSE Bitesize* at home, visit the website.

- Bring in a blank cassette and compile presentations on each topic.

- Work through exercises in *Das Stimmt/Bravo/Clarísimo.*

In turn we will do the following:

- Ensure you practise all four skill areas on the GCSE topics.

- Support you in the preparation of your coursework and your presentation for the oral.

- Give you feedback on how to improve and help you to set yourself targets to achieve the best possible grade.

- Offer extra speaking sessions before the oral exam period just after Easter.

- Supervise extra listening workshops in the Language Lab for you to practise GCSE listening questions.

- Show the BBC *GCSE Bitesize* revision video.

Source: Tile Hill Wood School and Language College

Pupil self assessment

It could be said that assessment is best done **with** pupils rather than just **to** or **by** them – surely if pupils have the ability to assess themselves it's the best possible situation! At least then they know how and what to improve.

Wiliam and Black's study (2002) showed that teachers working with ideas from their research involved pupils in setting and marking their tests. They found that getting pupils to comment on each other's work can have a substantial impact on learning. Firstly, pupils are better at spotting weaknesses in other people's work than their own. Secondly, pupils are much harder on each other than the teacher and can take criticism more easily from their peers than from the teacher. Furthermore, when misconceptions occur, explanations from classmates are often more effective than from the teacher, because they can interrupt when they have not grasped something and can ask for repeated explanations until it is clearly understood.

We can involve pupils in assessment by making learning objectives clear so that they understand what they are trying to achieve and by making assessment criteria transparent, discussing them in terms that pupils can understand. Depending on the type and purpose of the work and the feedback required, pupils can then be encouraged to assess their own work and others'. Self-assessment helps learners of foreign languages to develop the ability to identify their own weaknesses and difficulties, to understand where errors occur and how these might be avoided and to concentrate on specific linguistic details. Learning to see how elements of language fit in with each other and manipulating new language items or new structures in a familiar context are important steps in the process of foreign language learning. The skills of self-assessment, or becoming 'assessment literate', are an important part of developing into an independent learner. The example of a peer assessment sheet for oral work below alerts pupils to what they should be listening for when others perform, yet at the same time points to what is required in their own performance to reach a certain level.

Crib sheet for peer assessment of oral work: Level 5 and above

1 Which tense was the story in?
   - Past
   - Present
   - Future

2 Did you pick up any words which were time reference words?
   - Last week, yesterday, during the holidays, last weekend, last Saturday
   - Next week, tomorrow, during the holidays, next weekend, next Saturday
   - In the morning, in the afternoon, early, late, firstly, then, afterwards

3 Did you hear any opinions?
   - enjoyable, boring, expensive, too long, too loud, difficult, easy, etc.

4 Did you hear the speaker say **why** they have enjoyed/disliked (or will enjoy/dislike) the activities (e.g. were there some justifications?)

5 Did you pick out a physical description of a person, or a personality description?

6 Could you name the four activities undertaken (to be undertaken) by the speaker?

7 Did you understand the story clearly (e.g. pronunciation and intonation were very good/good/average/poor).

8 Did the speaker speak reasonably confidently, without relying on notes and was the pace good?

Source: Kineton High School

When teachers share with their students the process of assessment – giving up control, sharing power and leading students to take on the authority to assess themselves – the professional judgement of both is enhanced. Assessment becomes not something done to students. It becomes an activity done with students. (Brew, 1999: 169)

Peer- and self-assessment can also be of practical use to teachers, 'alleviating the assessment burden on the teacher' (Dickinson, 1987: 136), providing supplementary evidence and acting as an effective complement to tests and teacher assessment. In many cases self and peer assessment is a useful stage in preparation for teacher assessment. Pupils can check off the 'I can' statements themselves before being tested more formally on them. Of course, if pupils are marking their own or each other's written work, spot checks for accuracy are desirable! To benefit most from their foreign language study, pupils should always be engaged in self-checking activities, routinely testing themselves on vocabulary or carefully scrutinising their work before submitting it to the assessment of others. It is helpful to draw pupils' attention to major faults and try and encourage them into the habit of checking certain things before they hand work in, for example, in German, capital letters, word order, etc. As pupils progress, the checklist can become more sophisticated, for example, TAG: Tense (correct tense, verb ending), Agreement (adjectival endings), Gender.

Part of this self assessment involves pupils in taking responsibility for their own learning by keeping records of what they have achieved. Pupils could, for example, complete a 'My Work Diary'. This can help with class management, and involves pupils in self evaluation and target setting. It acts as a useful tool to discuss with pupils how much (or little!) they've done, and also can help with learning to learn.

My work diary

Name _____ Date _____

Date	Travail fini	Nom de l'exercice	C'est ...	Note
10.3.03	Oui	Qui est-ce?	Intéressant	8

Source: Languages for real purposes *by Julie Adams (Folens 2000), based on an idea by Peter Saunders.*

Equally, to present further challenge to pupils, they could be encouraged to keep a record of additional activities as a language learning log (see below).

Language learning log

Languages Teacher: ....

Name: ....

This form will help to remind you of the ways in which you can improve your skills. You should tick the boxes when you have completed the activities. Be honest with yourself! Your languages teacher will check this form every three weeks.

DATE

ACTIVITIES								
ATTENDED TUESDAY LUNCHTIME LISTENING								
LISTENED TO YOUR SPEAKING EXAM HELP TAPE								
SPEAKING PRACTICE WITH AN ASSISTANT								
WATCHED THE 'BITESIZE' VIDEO								
ATTENDED A LUNCHTIME HELP SESSION								
REVISED PRESENTATION								
ATTENDED EVERY LESSON								
LOOKED THROUGH EXERCISE BOOK/REVISED PARTICULAR AREA								
REVISED FROM NEAB GUIDE								

Source: Tile Hill Wood School and Language College

Similarly, pupils can be encouraged to maintain their own assessment records much as the teacher does. They can plot their progress to see how well they have performed in vocabulary tests, class and homework in different skill areas and end-of-module tests. Many coursebooks include photocopiable record sheets which could form part of this record. Again this encourages greater responsibility for their own learning and progress and can prove motivating.

Reflection Task

Pupil progress review

Have a look at the example (overleaf) of a progress review in languages.

- What do you think of this?
- Can you envisage some pupils you have taught benefiting from this approach?
- Look also at the Modern Languages review form on p87. This should be seen alongside the bank of targets in the section on target setting, p136.

Progress review in languages

Year _____

Date _____

Name _____

What have I achieved?	Targets set by me for the future

Next steps: agreed targets

What do I need to do to achieve these targets?

Questions to ask yourself:

- Have I worked to the best of my ability in lessons?
- Do I concentrate and listen during the lesson?
- Does my behaviour affect how I learn in lessons?
- Have I done anything during the lesson that has helped me to work well?
- Do I do my homework to the best of my ability?
- Do I hand in my homework on time?
- Do I learn Spanish words at home so it is easier for me to work in the class?
- If I do not understand anything do I turn for help to the teacher?

Source: President Kennedy School

Responding to pupils' work effectively

Modern Languages review

Name: _____

Date: _____

Main activities and assignments to date:

_____

_____

_____

_____

Which of these activities have you enjoyed the most and why?

_____

_____

_____

_____

Which of them have you found most difficult and why?

_____

_____

_____

_____

In what ways has your work got better this year?

_____

_____

_____

_____

What three things could you do now to improve your marks further?

_____

_____

_____

_____

Source: Tile Hill Wood School and Language College

Key points

- This chapter demonstrates the importance of responding to pupils' work effectively.

- While the marking of work is clearly significant, a mark in its own right is not especially helpful.

- We need to consider the type of work set to provide a sense of purpose, challenge and interest, and then ensure that selected tasks receive more detailed feedback on a regular basis.

- Feedback needs to be appropriate, specific and constructive.

- Part of this feedback involves setting targets of what and how to improve in order to raise attainment.

- Feedback, along with involving pupils in self assessment and review, encourages pupils to take greater responsibility for their learning.

5 Assessment across the age range and across the Attainment Targets

The importance of assessing pupils of all ages in all four skills has been made abundantly clear throughout this book. No matter what age the pupils are, being totally familiar with the assessment criteria is crucial to accurate assessment, and making these transparent to pupils will help to raise their achievement. This chapter concentrates initially on nationally-recognised criteria for assessing pupils at each key stage and then examines issues relating to assessing each of the Attainment Targets.

Assessment at KS3

Currently at Key Stage 3 pupils' learning and progress is characterised by the increasing expectations expressed in the National Curriculum level descriptions for each Attainment Target.

This assessment focuses on significant aspects of work, for example breadth of content and skills as outlined in the National Curriculum Programme of Study, as well as progress through the levels, and describes a pupil's performance in a range of work over a period of time. National Curriculum level descriptions were introduced to create an agreed understanding of standards, expectations and pupils' achievements in order to achieve consistency in teacher assessment.

 13

Trainee/NQT Task

National Curriculum level descriptions

Read through the NC level descriptions: you will need to become familiar with using these both in your planning and in your assessment of pupils' work. You can look up the QCA website and download the NC level descriptions: this makes it much easier to use them (cut and paste etc) in your planning and assessment. Look carefully to see how progression is characterised in each of the four skills.

The level descriptions are useful indicators for planning progression, some aspects of which may develop more quickly than others. For example, a pupil may progress more quickly in speaking than reading or writing. If we are aware of the level a pupil is working at, we can monitor progress through the levels by setting targets of what needs to be achieved to reach the next level. One task may provide evidence of achievement in more than one AT (e.g. a writing task may involve a substantial amount of reading). It is reasonable to expect that some KS3 pupils in Years 8 and 9 attain Levels 5 or 6 or even 7. Challenging pupils to meet the higher levels of the National Curriculum should be built in where appropriate. The KS3 Framework in MFL has the potential to transform teaching and learning at KS3 with greater focus on knowledge about language and emphasis on progression. The level descriptions need to be viewed as representing continuous development:

> *Pupils' progress is also restricted where insufficient opportunities are provided to develop the strands running through the level descriptions of Attainment Targets 2 and 4. Not all strands are referred to explicitly at every level, but their development should be continuous. For example, a key indicator of pupils' ability to cope is contained in AT2 at Level 6: 'They [pupils] use the target language to meet most of their routine needs for information and explanation'. This is flagged at Level 2, where they are expected to use set phrases to ask for help and permission. Although the strand is not explicit in Levels 3–5, it has to be built up over Key Stage 3. In AT4, drawing on using language from memory when writing is overtly stated at Levels 2 and 3 but not thereafter, and yet it is a prerequisite for functioning at the high levels (for example, Level 6 'they apply grammar in new contexts'.)* (OFSTED 2002b)

It is a statutory requirement to report pupils' levels for the Foundation Language at the end of KS3. Levels are teacher assessed; there are no national tests at the end of KS3. The National Curriculum for Modern Foreign Languages (DfES and QCA 1999) included modifications to certain level descriptions to enable the majority of pupils to attain Level 5 or 6 at the end of the key stage in line with other subjects. Generally, levels are not awarded to individual pieces of work, but instead teachers make a rounded judgement at the end of KS3, based on their knowledge of how the pupil performs in a range of contexts: a 'best fit' approach in each Attainment Target for the particular individual.

If assessment is to be continuous and an integral part of teaching and learning, it is better perhaps not to view the levels as fences to be jumped but instead fields in which a pupil might be working. This avoids the trap of misinterpreting a pupil's progression on the basis of a limited range of work.

Field A	Field B	Field C
Level 4	Level 5	Level 6

For example, a pupil **can** work in all three fields but, at the end of the year or the Key Stage, in which field does he or she work most of the time? You can conclude that in the latter part of the Key Stage, whichever level the pupil was mostly in is the level to which he or she is most suited.

Awarding a level at the end of KS3 should be on the basis of your professional judgement. It should take into account:

- close reference to the level description;
- your knowledge of how the pupil performs across a range of contexts;
- the different strengths and weaknesses of the pupil's performance in each AT.

The following example of assessment at the end of Key Stage 3 is from the Tile Hill Wood School and Language College assessment policy (see also Appendix 4).

Teacher assessment of our students' overall performance at the end of KS3 refers to a body of work produced over the year by the student. This can include levels given to classwork, homework and unit tests, as well as to performance in class. Students' work may 'show characteristics of Level …', a student may be 'working towards Level …' or she may have 'given evidence of performance at Level …'. However, attainment should be sustained over a period of time. Our judgement is based on a range of pieces of work and performance in class in a variety of contexts. We need to give the most appropriate level in each skill following the 'best fit' idea, checking against adjacent levels. Performance may well be uneven across the Attainment Targets. To support us in our judgements, we have the original SCAA tapes and booklets 'Exemplification of standards' and the more recent updating on the QCA website **www.qca.org.uk**.

Source: Tile Hill Wood School and Language College

To help teachers allocate levels consistently, SCAA produced *MFL: Consistency in teacher assessment. Exemplification of standards: Key Stage 3.* This material is being updated to be in line with the new level descriptions. It would be useful for trainees to use these materials initially to familiarise themselves with the levels allocated to pupils' work. Once in school, they will be able to work alongside the mentor and other members of the department to develop their skills further in judging pupils' work.

 14

Trainee/NQT Task

Using the exemplification of standards materials

The SCAA MFL/KS3 Exemplification of standards booklet and cassette provide examples of pupils' work and how levels have been allocated to these. In examining the material, bear in mind that this was originally published in June 1996 and consequently there are differences with the NC 2000 levels. These materials are now available on-line at the QCA website.

• Look at selected pieces of work and mark them yourself and then compare your findings with those in the booklet.

In Autumn 1996/Spring 1997 SCAA devised packs of KS3 optional tests and tasks in French, German and Spanish as exemplar material for use in schools, to promote consistency in teacher assessment. These have been amended in the light of NC 2000 and are available from **www.qca.org.uk/ca/subjects/mfl** and can be inserted into the original booklets.

The rationale behind producing these tests and tasks is:

■ to assist teachers in making consistent judgements on pupils' attainment based on agreed national standards;
■ to provide examples of appropriate methods of assessing MFL in KS3;
■ to provide information that can contribute to an end of key stage judgement of pupils' attainment in MFL;
■ to provide information about pupils which may be used to plan further learning objectives.

As there is no intention to have statutory tests for MFL, the optional tests and tasks help to standardise departmental judgements. For example, all teachers could use the test with all groups and then come back together and moderate their marking to achieve consistency across the department. There are no plans to publish MFL KS3 results by school. The department should collect overall statistics. The levels are reported to parents for comparison, but also provide records for departmental management, for example, comparing results for top/middle/bottom sets.

15

Trainee/NQT Task

Using the optional tests and tasks materials

Familiarise yourself with one of the topic booklets of the optional tests and analyse what you find. Each unit deals with all four Attainment although the emphasis might vary. The tasks cover Levels 1–8, but particular focus is given to Levels 2–6, the expected range for the majority of KS3 pupils. What level would you allocate to the tasks?

- As you make your decisions, try to focus on your first impressions of the pack as a whole, then choose one of the tests to look at in detail and give a critical analysis of:
  - the task itself;
  - level;
  - visuals;
  - layout;
  - rubrics;
  - authentic materials;
  - teacher's notes;
  - assessment criteria;
  - ease of use;
  - pupils' possible reactions – motivating?

- Ask yourself:
  - would this have been appropriate for your classes?
  - would this help you to assess your pupils?
  - are there any disadvantages?

A model of departmental good practice with KS3 assessment is exemplified by Cardinal Wiseman RC School (see pp92–93).

- The department has collected a Portfolio of evidence showing examples of marked pupils' work in each Attainment Target with an explanation of the task and best fit level awarded as a reference point for teachers, NQTs and trainees.

- MFL teachers keep AT level descriptions reduced to A5 size in the front of their mark books for quick reference.

- AT level descriptions in pupil-friendly language (see pp92–93) are posted on all classroom walls so that pupils can refer to them.

Pupil-friendly level descriptions

Level	AT1: Listening and Responding
1	You can understand *basic* classroom commands, short statements and questions, which are spoken *clearly and slowly*. You may need *some repetition or gestures* to help you.
2	You can understand *a range of* familiar statements and questions, including everyday classroom language and instructions for doing your work. The language used must be spoken clearly and slowly. You may need some items to be repeated.
3	You can understand *short passages* of familiar language spoken at *near normal speed*. You can pick out *main points and personal responses*, such as likes and dislikes. You may need some items to be repeated.
4	You can understand *longer passages*, made up of familiar language and spoken at near normal speed. You can pick out *main points and some details*. You may need some items to be repeated.
5	You can understand longer passages, made up of familiar language from *several topics*, including *past, present and future events* and spoken at near normal speed. You can pick out *main points and specific details*, including opinions. You may need some repetition.
6	You can understand extracts of spoken language drawn from *a variety of topics*, spoken at near normal speed and *with some interference*. You can pick out main points and specific details, including points of view. You need *little repetition*.

Level	AT2: Speaking
1	You can respond to what you see or hear with *single words* or a short phrase. Your *pronunciation* may still be *approximate* and you need considerable help from your teacher or other people on a tape when learning new words.
2	You can give *short, simple responses* to what you see and hear. You can *name and describe people, places and objects*. You can *ask for help or permission* to do something. You may be a little hesitant, but *your meaning is clear*.
3	You can take part in a *short prepared conversation of at least two or three exchanges*. You can talk about your likes, dislikes and preferences. Although you use mainly memorised language, you occasionally *substitute single words* to vary questions or statements.
4	You can take part in a simple structured conversation of *at least three or four exchanges*. You can *substitute* single words and *phrases*. Although your *pronunciation* is generally *accurate* and your *intonation* is quite good, eg. you raise your voice at the end of a question.
5	You can take part in short conversations in which *you refer to recent experiences and future plans*, as well as everyday activities and interests. Although you make *some mistakes*, you can *make yourself understood with little or no difficulty*.
6	You are becoming able to improvise a conversation with a partner in which you talk about past, present and future actions. You may be *hesitant at times*, but you can *make yourself understood with little or no difficulty*.

Source: Cardinal Wiseman School

Assessment across the age range and across the Attainment Targets

Level	AT3: Reading and Responding
1	You can understand *single words* written clearly.
2	You can understand *short phrases* about topics you have covered. You can *read aloud familiar words and phrases*. You can use *a dictionary or a glossary* in your text book to look up new words.
3	You can understand *short passages* about topics you have covered if they are printed or word processed. You can pick out *main points*, including likes, dislikes and feelings. You have *started to read on your own* with the help of your dictionary.
4	You can understand **the main points and some details** in a short story or factual piece of writing which is *printed or clearly handwritten*. You do not always have to rely on a dictionary - *you can work out the meaning of some unfamiliar words for yourself*.
5	You can understand the *main points and specific details*, including opinions, *in different kinds of writing* eg. information leaflets, magazine articles or *hand written* letters, which mention past, present and future events. You are *more confident about reading aloud and using a dictionary*.
6	You can understand *a variety of texts* that include familiar language in unfamiliar contexts. You can *scan magazines or books* for items of interest to you and to see if the language used is at the right level for you. You are becoming *more confident in working out the meaning of unfamiliar words* using context and grammatical understanding.

Level	AT4: Writing
1	You can *copy single words* correctly. You can select appropriate words to complete short phrases or sentences.
2	You can *copy short phrases* correctly. When you write familiar words from memory you may *still make spelling mistakes*.
3	You can write *2 or 3 short sentences*, using your exercise book, textbook or wallcharts to help you. You can write about your *likes and dislikes*. You can write *short phrases from memory with reasonable spelling*.
4	You can write a paragraph of *3 or 4 sentences* largely from memory. You can *substitute individual words or phrases* in a model answer. You are beginning *to use a dictionary or the glossary* in your textbook to help you.
5	You can produce short pieces of writing in which you refer to past, *present and future events*. You try to apply the *grammar* you have been taught, but may still make *a number of mistakes*.
6	You can write *in paragraphs* and refer to past, present and future actions. You can use both *formal and informal styles* of writing, such as writing a letter to book accommodation or writing a letter to a friend. You make *some mistakes, but the meaning is usually clear*.

Source: Cardinal Wiseman School

Assessment across the age range and across the Attainment Targets

Pupil-friendly level descriptions

Many departments have developed their own pupil-friendly versions of the NC level descriptions. This is a way of making pupils more familiar with what constitutes a particular level and enables them to improve their work by including the necessary detail to reach a higher level.

Trainee/NQT Task

Using pupil-friendly level descriptions

Referring constantly to the NC levels can be difficult and tiring. Encapsulating key words in each level is much simpler. On pp92–93 and in Appendix 5 you will find some examples from different schools of the NC level descriptions rewritten for pupils in pupil-friendly terms, so they can work on improving their achievements and know what to aim for. Become familiar with these too. Keep them next to you when you are marking pupils' work.

Some departments are already seeking alternative accreditation for use with Year 9 pupils and this pattern seems likely to grow in order to encourage motivation to continue through Year 9 given the curriculum changes where the statutory requirement to continue a Modern Foreign Language to sixteen is likely to be relaxed. The proposed national recognition scheme or language ladder of progression (one of the overarching objectives of *Languages for all: languages for life,* DfES, 2003) may offer alternative recognition for learning in the future.

Assessment at KS4

In the light of the Green Paper: *14–19 extending opportunities, raising standards* (DfES 2002) statutory requirements are changing for MFL. While for some years the study of MFL was compulsory at both KS3 and KS4, MFL is now to be optional at KS4. Assessment at KS4 naturally tends to be exam dominated with accreditation at the end of KS4 being in the main GCSE (linear or modular) or Entry Level Certificate.

New GCSE subject criteria are being examined from 2003. The revisions are to bring GCSE into line with the revised National Curriculum 2000. The principles are the same as those underlying the new NC and the QCA Scheme of Work. Many aspects remain similar:

- Foundation and Higher Tiers are retained with equal weighting across the four language skills. Foundation Tier targets grades G to C; Higher Tier targets grades D to A*. Coursework, with no tiers, is differentiated by outcome.
- Examinations draw on authentic materials and some texts are based on ICT sources, for example e-mail messages will feature in writing papers and authentic texts may come from a website.
- Normally instructions are in the Target Language, except where the nature of the task would make them difficult to understand.
- Maximum 5% for English responses in listening and reading.

However, there is a shift away from topics linked to specific Key Stages towards pupils' knowledge of language and their ability to apply it in a variety of contexts. To reinforce this greater emphasis on understanding of language structure and grammar:

- tasks will continue to have a clear **communicative** purpose but there will be

Assessment across the age range and across the Attainment Targets

a **premium on using appropriate structures and achieving a high degree of accuracy**;

- in Speaking and Writing at least 10% of marks in each skill must be allocated to knowledge and accurate application of the **grammar and structures** of the foreign language – and these marks will all be concentrated in speaking and writing tests (but not an introduction of decontextualised tests of grammar);
- content (grammar and structures) is specified for Higher and Foundation Tiers, and vocabulary is specified for Foundation Tier;
- from 2003, **dictionaries will no longer be available** in exams, but pupils will be encouraged to use dictionaries for coursework and general language learning purposes.

This should have a significant effect on the way all candidates are taught, especially at Foundation level.

The Modular GCSE has also undergone changes alongside the linear GCSE. Initially many teachers saw the advantages of modular GCSE as:

- relevance of the material to the learner;
- the ability it offered to create an 'authentic' audience;
- room for creative project work, including learners making cassettes about themselves;
- progress could be regularly and easily measured;
- pupils had the opportunity to work up through the levels and to submit only their best work;
- there was no exam stress because assessments were carried out in class when the pupil was ready;
- for poor attenders, assessments could be 'caught up on';
- pupils did not have to 'perform' well on a particular day.

When the regulations were changed for examination in 1998, 50% of the final grade was based on terminal assessment. Many teachers found this, along with the huge marking and administration load, detracted from its attractiveness as an alternative.

The Certificate of Achievement, aimed at NC Levels 2/3 has been developed to cater for pupils who are considered unlikely to be successful in achieving a GCSE grade. The Certificate of Achievement has 12 units and pupils build up a portfolio of evidence which is moderated by the examining group. For many students recognition of their achievement at the end of each unit of work is a motivating factor. From 2003 this is included in the new Entry Level Certificates.

GCSE examinations

The following websites include the complete specifications, specimen question papers, assessment criteria and mark schemes and in some cases support materials, e.g. coursework exemplar materials, speaking and writing materials and vocabulary lists.

- **www.edexcel.org.uk** (EdExcel Examining Group site)
- **www.ocr.org.uk** (OCR Examining Group site)
- **www.neab.ac.uk** (AQA Examining Group site)

17

Trainee/NQT Task

Examining groups

When you are in school, find out which examining group is used and make yourself more familiar with the details of the specifications, sample papers, past exam papers, etc.

 18

Trainee/NQT Task

Learning from a GCSE paper

- Familiarise yourself with the requirements of the GCSE. Obtain a recent GCSE exam in your FL1 or FL2. Complete the paper as if you were a pupil and stick to correct procedures (e.g. time limit, number of words, etc).

- Afterwards ask yourself:
  – what (if anything) did you find difficult?
  – what have you learnt about **a)** strategies you need to help the pupils develop and **b)** language issues?

As with KS3, accurate assessment at KS4 requires total familiarity with task types and assessment criteria. While not all work will necessarily be marked according to these criteria, it is important to mark key pieces of work at regular intervals according to the criteria. This helps to familiarise both teacher and pupil with content, style of test types and assessment criteria in order to explore ways of improving work to reach higher grades. To ensure consistency across a department it is useful to collate and moderate examples of different standards of work and discuss these as a department. The following task provides one way of achieving greater familiarity with assessment criteria.

 12

Reflection Task

GCSE grade descriptors

Look at the GCSE grade descriptors opposite. How would they:

- help pupils improve their own work?

- help you in your planning, teaching and assessment?

Jo Redford, Head of Department, has the following suggestions for using the pupil-friendly grade descriptions:

- link the descriptions to real pieces of work;
- bullet point them and split them up, then ask pupils to recombine each statement according to the correct skill and grade;
- pupils assess their own and anonymous pieces of work;
- integrate the descriptions into lesson objectives;
- ask pupils to match various descriptions to the appropriate skill.

Preparing pupils effectively for exams by planning learning objectives carefully, giving access to past papers or exam-style tasks, sharing criteria and what needs to be done to achieve improvement, helping pupils to develop learning strategies and revision techniques are all crucial and can make a real difference to results. The revision tips on p98 are a way of encouraging pupils to think about what they can do themselves to improve their chances of a good result.

**Modern Languages: GCSE grade descriptors
2003**

Listening

Grade F: I can identify and note **main points** and pick out **some details from simple language** spoken clearly **at near normal speed.**

Grade C: I can identify and note main points and pick out details and **points of view** from language spoken at **normal speed.** The **spoken passages** include past and future events. They are drawn from a variety of topics which include **language I know in new contexts.**

Grade A: I can **understand gist** and pick out main points and detail in a **variety of types of authentic spoken language.** I am able to recognise points of view, **attitudes and emotions** and I can **draw conclusions.**

Reading

Grade F: I can identify and note **main points** and pick out **some information from short, simple texts.** I can **use context to work out the meaning** of words.

Grade C: I can identify and note main points and **pick out details and points of view** from a range of texts, drawn from a variety of topics and which include **past, present and future** events. I am able to **understand unfamiliar language.**

Grade A: I **understand gist** and recognise main points and detail in a variety of authentic texts. I recognise points of view, **attitudes and emotions** and I am able to **draw conclusions.** I can understand unfamiliar and **more complex language.**

Speaking

Grade F: I can take part in simple conversations showing **some ability to substitute words and phrases. My pronunciation is generally accurate,** and although **there may be grammatical mistakes,** I communicate the main points.

Grade C: I can develop conversations and simple discussions referring to **past, present and future events,** using different tenses. **I can express personal opinions** and I am able to deal with **some unpredictable elements.** Although there **may be some errors,** my message is clear, and **my pronunciation and intonation are generally accurate.**

Grade A: I can start and develop conversations and discussions, and describe events. I can express and **give reasons for my ideas** and points of view, and **produce longer sentences** using a variety of vocabulary, structures and verb tenses. I speak confidently, with **good pronunciation and intonation.** The message is clear although there **may still be some errors, especially when I use more complex structures.**

Writing

Grade F: I can write **short sentences,** and respond to written texts by **substituting words and set phrases.** Although there may be **mistakes in my spelling and grammar, I communicate the main points.**

Grade C: I can **express personal opinions** and write about a variety of topics, both factually and **imaginatively,** including **past, present and future events** and using different tenses. My style is basic but appropriate. Despite **some errors** my writing conveys a clear message.

Grade A: I can write information and **describe events** both factually and imaginatively. I can express and **give reasons** for my ideas and points of view. I am able to **produce longer sentences** using a range of vocabulary, structure and verb tenses. My **spelling and grammar are generally accurate,** and my style is appropriate to the purpose.

Source: Tile Hill Wood School and Language College

Tips for effective exam preparation: what will make the difference for you?

- Willing attitude in class to listen carefully and 'have a go', follow the advice of your teacher, be organised and conscientious with homework.

- Start revision early: get all exercise books together, look over each topic, highlight, condense down to the essential, revise key phrases and vocabulary.

- Buy the exam guides on offer.

- Use our facilities: room 41 is reserved just for you every Wednesday lunchtime with loads of software for role-play practice and the excellent website: **www.bbc.co.uk/education/revision.**

- GCSE *Bitesize* TV programmes: bring in a blank video to get your own copy, use the new books which go with the programme ...

- Grab the opportunity to do extra speaking practice with the assistant, support teacher.

- Prepare a presentation with prompts for your mock speaking exam in December.

- Use the general conversation booklets to rehearse your answers for the general conversation section of the oral. Remember the importance of volunteering extra information.

- Follow advice with course work. Try hard to include all three tenses, opinions and reasons. Check your writing for silly mistakes. Meet the deadlines.

- Get extra reading practice by completing reading homeworks from *Das Stimmt/Bravo/Clarísimo.*

Source: Tile Hill Wood School and Language College

Assessing across the Attainment Targets

Within this broad picture of rising attainment, the majority of pupils continue to show weaknesses in one or more of the four main MFL skills of listening, speaking, reading and writing. The balance of weaknesses varies from school to school. Some reports indicate, for example, that listening and speaking are weaker than reading and writing and others the reverse. Considerable improvement could be brought about in individual schools if the MFL departments sought to achieve greater consistency across these aspects of the subject. (OFSTED 2002b)

It is important to assess all Attainment Targets and maintain a record of pupils' attainment in a meaningful, clear way to create a cumulative picture of individual pupils' progress in each Attainment Target. This might be achieved by colour coding each AT or recording each AT in separate columns or on separate pages in your mark book. Using assessment formatively rather than relying too heavily on end-of-unit tests will help in building up this picture. Creating opportunities to assess at higher levels will also ensure pupils are enabled to reach their potential. What do the pupils think?:

 *I think tests in Modern Languages are ...*

- *fairly hard in writing and speaking but easy in reading and listening.* (Girl, 13)
- *for learning to speak, read and listen in French.* (Girl, 12)
- *good as they test you in all three ways – reading, writing and speaking.* (Girl, 15)

Assessing Attainment Target 1: listening & responding

My Modern Languages teacher helps me learn best when ...

- *we listen to tapes. (Girl, 11)*
- *doing tape tests so I learn more French. (Boy, 12)*
- *we listen to the tapes and write the answers. (Boy, 12)*
- *I'm listening to tapes and writing stuff down and in a good mood. (Girl, 12)*

Pupils listen to a range of inputs: their teacher, each other, cassettes, video, guests, TV, CD-ROM, radio, songs. The most common source apart from the teacher is likely to be a tape: it gives pupils a chance to hear a native speaker model and to hear the kind of language they might hear when abroad. Most often heard are tapes accompanying courses, but schools may also have access to authentic speech as in tapes from a partner class or made by the teacher or even pupils recording messages for each other. Summative and external assessment usually use taped materials, and classroom practice is therefore vital, both for listening to learn, (to develop language competence) and learning to listen (to develop listening skills). There are some inherent difficulties about taped materials: anonymity, extraneous noises, demands on memory, lack of external orientation and speed of delivery. Listening in a foreign language is much more difficult: the support systems are missing (there is no here-and-now, no concrete setting) and when listening to recorded material there is no facial expression, no body language and therefore no additional supports to reach a negotiated meaning.

Developing pupil confidence in listening requires training in listening skills, for example, familiarity with difficult sounds in the target language, an understanding of the sound-spelling link, identifying and differentiating sounds and structures, marker words, prediction and brainstorming language from the title. Encouraging pupils to think about listening strategies will also help: understand the question set, the kind of question it is (is it asking for details, or for an overall impression?) looking for useful clues in the question or what they listen to. Allowing pupils to listen individually at their own pace so that they can rewind the tape and listen as many times as they need is especially helpful when preparing for examinations.

Assessing listening can be informal, for example, how learners respond to instructions in the target language or how they interpret language in pairwork as well as whole-class activities. Examples of listening tasks which could be used for more formal assessment include:

- listening for how often something is said;
- distinguishing between sounds;
- listening for specific items of vocabulary;
- true/false statements;
- listening to the order in which something is said;
- matching pictures/symbols to what is heard;
- filling in categories on a grid;
- gap fill activities in the target language text or in an English summary from what they hear;
- ticking or crossing a list of facilities a hotel may have depending on what they hear;
- matching information to what they hear, e.g. allocating the best person to a job;
- drawing or completing a picture or diagram using taped text as a prompt;
- multiple choice;
- target language question/answer;
- English question/answer;

Assessment across the age range and across the Attainment Targets

- following instructions or plotting a route on a map;
- matching headlines with the order of heard material;
- spotting grammatical features, e.g. a specific tense or structure.

Responses to the listening task can combine with other skills, for example taking notes or writing a summary in the target language or reporting orally what has been heard.

Factors to consider when assessing AT1

- Type of question.
- Informal, ongoing assessment (how pupils respond to instructions in the target language, how they use language in pairwork as well as whole-class activities).
- Formal testing.
- Balance between comprehension and 'overloading' of the memory.
- Listen and draw and/or listen and do.

Assessing Attainment Target 2: speaking

Interestingly when we asked pupils how their teacher helped them learn best, **speaking** featured in many responses:

My Modern Languages teacher helps me learn best when ...

- *playing games – speaking. (Girl, 14)*
- *he plays games to help you learn words. (Girl, 14)*
- *we have to learn how to pronounce French. (Girl, 14)*
- *she gets us to repeat. (Girl, 12)*
- *she talks out loud and so do we. (Boy, 12)*
- *she tells us to repeat after her. (Boy, 12)*
- *I am speaking French. (Boy, 13)*
- *we are doing speaking exercises. (Girl, 12)*
- *I'm talking in French. (Girl, 11)*
- *I speak it. (Girl, 12)*
- *she does oral lessons so I can experience talking it. (Girl, 15)*

Pupils were also quite positive about the value of tests with regard to speaking:

I think tests in Modern Languages are ...

- *useful because if you go abroad you can speak it. (Girl, 12)*
- *important for communicating with other people. (Boy, 12)*
- *quite hard but very helpful and improve my speaking and writing a lot. (Boy, 14)*
- *a reassuring way of knowing how fluent you are. (Boy, 15)*

However, pupil responses also indicated that speaking is the skill they often find most difficult:

I think tests in Modern Languages are ...

- *quite difficult, especially the speaking. (Girl, 13)*
- *quite difficult if it is a speaking test because of the amount we have to learn. (Boy, 16)*
- *good but I think there is too much for speaking to revise. (Girl, 16)*

> • *hard to understand – especially the pronunciation.*
>   (Girl, 15)
> • *reasonably hard – especially learning for speaking.*
>   (Girl, 15)

While there has been greater emphasis on speaking and listening in lessons to reflect both NC Attainment Targets and GCSE equal weighting of skills, speaking still remains the most neglected skill as far as assessment is concerned. Yet, unless it is assessed regularly, pupils can undervalue speaking as they often think the 'real' work only starts when pen and paper are involved. Assessing speaking regularly also makes pupils aware of their own standard and how they can progress. For example, errors in speaking, such as pronunciation, don't simply need correcting: pupils need to know why it is wrong and how to get it right in the future.

Assessment of speaking tasks can readily be incorporated into normal lessons, employing the usual teaching materials and activities. These should be designed specifically to stimulate interactive communication, preferably including elements of unpredictability. One-to-one speaking tests conducted by the teacher can take up considerable class time, leaving other pupils perhaps working without support. It is therefore helpful to devise a system of assessing pupils through observation and eavesdropping of pairs performing a structured or unstructured role-play, an interview, or discussion of a topic, or assessing a playlet or sketch, mini-talk or presentation to the group. If pupils are conducting a survey, the teacher could be one of the compulsory five people to be interviewed. A real life information-gap activity in which pupils seek and provide information, for example in arranging a meeting after discussing alternative opportunities and prior commitments, or exchanging information about leisure facilities, provides a natural opportunity to communicate.

The advantages of ongoing assessment of this kind while learners are working at the activities are clear:

- pupils will feel less nervous because, rather than a 'test', the activity forms part of a normal lesson;
- pupils work in pairs or small groups in a relaxed atmosphere;
- the teacher can listen, observe and evaluate pupils' competence;
- the activity is task-based and uses authentic language;
- the task can be multi-skill, for example passing on a phone message, so that pupils note down elements of what they hear as part of the task, providing additional evidence of competence to back up teacher observation.

Suggestions for assessing speaking

- You could incorporate space in your markbook for TL use in class by pupils.
- With some classes, you could develop peer/partner observations/analysis of each other's speaking.
- Give speaking homeworks where pupils record themselves on cassette; you as the teacher report back on tape, give pronunciation help, etc.
- You could have an exercise book for each class with a page per child to enter informal assessment information gained in class, particularly with regard to assessing speaking;
- Make sure you clarify **exactly** what you're looking for and therefore what they need to work on, e.g. pronunciation, use of language, intonation, etc.
- You could video pupils and ask them to 'critique' their performance (according to the clear criteria).

Factors to consider when assessing AT2

- One-to-one 'chat' – where? how? (given numbers and time) – but gives shy pupils a better chance, could tape them and mark later.
- Subjective grading based on normal class output.
- 'Stretching' brighter pupils (creating 'real-life' info gap through unexpected answers).
- Credit for **comprehension**.

**Trainee/NQT
Task**

Conducting a GCSE speaking test

Try to arrange with your mentor to 'conduct' a GCSE speaking test with one or two pupils. You could use this to help pupils prepare. Treat it as a 'proper' test, i.e. follow the correct instructions regarding time for preparation, conduct of the test, etc. Make sure you record the results (as you would in the real thing). Afterwards, ask yourself the following questions and discuss them with your mentor:

- What did you find challenging?

- Do you think you enabled the pupils to show what they could do (i.e. achieve their potential)?

- What would you do differently next time?

Providing pupils with a structure for their speaking test, including a checklist of essential items, is a useful way of helping pupils know how to score highly. The example below shows the presentation section of a GCSE speaking test.

Preparing my presentation	
Name: Date:	
Communication • I have said the name of the popstar at the beginning of the presentation. • I have given 3 reasons why I like them. • I have described 2 things about them. • I have chosen a good phrase to finish off. • I have used some interesting pictures. • I have practised my presentation so I don't have to read from my notes.	
Language • I have checked that I have used the right tenses. • I have used different ways of giving my opinion. • I have used linking words like 'because' and 'although'.	
Strategies • I have used this grid to make sure my presentation is clear, interesting and accurate. • I have used reference books to help me (dictionary, grammar book, other).	
After my partner listened to me, this is what I have done to make my presentation better:	

Source: Vee Harris 2002 (adapted from Vandergrift 1999)

Assessment across the age range and across the Attainment Targets

Have a look at the GCSE General Conversation Exam feedback sheets that follow. These have been filled in by the teacher after practice GCSE speaking tests. A similar sheet completed by the Spanish FLA provides feedback to pupils about a telephone conversation. There is also the *prueba* report which is completed jointly by the pupil and the teacher.

GCSE GENERAL CONVERSATION EXAM

Keep up the good work. Clear evidence of progress.

Name:		Comment
Communication (0–4)	2+	*Some answers developed.*
Spontaneity & Fluency (0–4)	3	*You volunteered information which is good. Some prompting needed in places.*
Quality of language Range and complexity (0–6)	3+	*Past tense successfully used. Keep working on the future: voy a ver ...*
Pronunciation and accuracy (0–6)	3+	*Remember: Cómo es = what is ... like? Tiene 38 años (not 'es')*
Total: 20	11	

Source: Tile Hill Wood School and Language College

GCSE GENERAL CONVERSATION EXAM

Name:		Comment
Communication (0–4)	3	*Questions understood and answers given.*
Spontaneity & Fluency (0–4)	3	*You sometimes volunteered extra information.*
Quality of language Range and complexity (0–6)	3	*Good use of 'Quisiera ser periodista' but past tense endings not used successfully. Remember you need to change the verb ending to 'I' form in your answer. On one occasion you corrected yourself – Estás to estoy – good.*
Pronunciation and accuracy (0–6)	3	*Take care: inglés iglesia*
Total: 20	12	

Source: Tile Hill Wood School and Language College

Assessment across the age range and across the Attainment Targets

GCSE GENERAL CONVERSATION EXAM

Name:

Source: Tile Hill Wood School and Language College

		Comment
Communication (0–4)	2	Don't get into the habit of translating the questions out loud into English. Clear evidence of progress.
Spontaneity & Fluency (0–4)	2	Ready responses but I would like you to take the initiative and offer extra information/detail/reason.
Quality of language Range and complexity (0–6)	3	Work on using the past/future accurately.
Pronunciation and accuracy (0–6)	3	Check how to pronounce : el cine, la pista de hielo.
Total: 20	10	

Una llamada telefónica con Rosa
Nombre :

el saludo	
la invitación	
la fecha	
el viaje	
unas actividades	
El fin de la conversación	
otro	
la pronunciación/fluidez	

Source: Tile Hill Wood School and Language College

Assessment across the age range and across the Attainment Targets

Prueba el 15 de Octobre

	Name:
Fluency/ memory	(New partners). Very good.
Pronunciation Do I Sound Spainsh?	Muchos gracias. Muchas
Grammatical accuracy	es. → está. Confusion with time
Content	✓ ✓ ✓ ✓ ✓
Level (2-5)	level 5 ~ just!
Target	You have worked hard for this test. Well done! Keep up your efforts.

> You answered really well during today's lesson.
> Well done! Mrs J Redford

Source: Tile Hill Wood School and Language College

Assessment across the age range and across the Attainment Targets

Speaking skills in KS3: the Head of Department's perspective

The following section is written from the perspective of Jo Redford, Head of Department at Tile Hill Wood School and Language College in Coventry (see also Appendix 4).

> Speaking tests are also a regular feature of our assessment in all key stages. Role plays, mini presentations and question/answer work may be conducted between teacher–pupil, pupil–pupil or assistant–pupil and may or may not be taped as necessary. It is helpful to make a few notes at the time of the oral on aspects such as pronunciation, communication, accuracy, etc in order to give written feedback on an individual basis to students.
>
> *Source: Tile Hill Wood School and Language College*

Many pupils think that speaking is unimportant and that the real work only starts when writing is given. Therefore in my department we give the skill of speaking status by impressing on pupils that speaking is a transferable skill and is helpful in developing social and communication skills. Pupils' effort is recognised by the use of praise, stickers and merits.

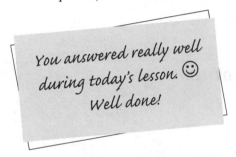

A variety of activities is used, for example a soft ball thrown to individual pupils to focus response, the use of a microphone, flashcards, realia (for example, a suitcase of children's clothes or a shopping bag filled with plastic fruit), a stopwatch to extend conversation on topics. Videos of individuals, pairs or groups can be motivating and inspire pupils to produce a high standard of work.

In order to improve speaking skills, levels of answer are demonstrated:

- *Tu as des frères ou des sœurs?*
- *Oui, j'ai un frère.*
- *Oui, j'ai un frère qui s'appelle …*
- *Oui, j'ai un frère qui s'appelle … Il aime le football.*

It is important to search for more conceptually demanding material to entice students out of routine answers. In order to improve pupils' achievements in speaking assessments pupils are provided with a **'menu'** of what should be included for a mini presentation, for example:

Year 8: a weekend away in the past

- A description of place, accommodation, and weather.
- Details of some activities.
- A range of subjects – *nous, on, je, il/elle.*
- Expressions of time.
- Opinions.

As in the GCSE presentation pupils are allowed prompt cards.

Written feedback on the speaking assessment helps pupils to focus both on their achievement and elements they can improve, for example:

> **Year 8 speaking test: a holiday**
>
> Level 5+ good detail in your description of a holiday in a *village de vacances*. Accurate past tenses with a range of subjects and good expressions of time. Well done! Note: pronunciation of *dans* (silent *'s'*), *nous **avons** joué au tennis, je pense **que** ma semaine **était** fantastique.*

To extend speaking skills at KS3, departmental planning includes extending the textbook to NC Level 6. Speaking skills are further extended in KS4 by:

- open-ended questions (how many facts can you provide in 'x' time? stopwatch);
- transference of language across topics;
- building phrases around a picture;
- predicting the language for a given situation;
- dealing with the 'unpredictable';
- use of the assistants and native speakers;
- practice on the software;
- tapes with general conversation questions;
- extra small group practice sessions;
- practice of essential verbs in a range of tenses.

Pupils are encouraged to take the initiative and improve their answers by including longer sentences and more complex structures. Teachers share examples of possible responses with pupils and encourage them to highlight the differences. In this way they can see how to improve their answer and so improve their grade, for example:

> ***Comment vas-tu au collège?***
>
> - *A pied*
> - *Je vais au collège à pied.*
> - *J'y vais à pied parce que j'habite assez près du collège.*
> - *Normalement j'y vais à pied parce que j'habite assez près, mais hier, comme il pleuvait j'ai pris l'autobus.*

Our departmental marking policy at Tile Hill Wood School and Language College includes the following on speaking (see also Appendix 1):

> Given the importance of speaking in the Modern Languages classroom, it is important to give **feedback on a student's participation,** pronunciation, willingness to enter a role, to extend her answers in class and performance in speaking tests. This may be in the form of a written comment in exercise books or a department slip issued during the course of the lesson in recognition of progress with speaking skills. Students are to stick these in their exercise books.
>
> *Source: Tile Hill Wood School and Language College*

Finally, we have a series of tips we provide for pupils – tips for success in your speaking exam.

Tips for success in your speaking exam

In addition to full attention and maximum effort in lessons, revise for the three sections – role play, presentation, general conversation – following the tips below. Remember you will be marked on four aspects: the content of what you say, the variety and accuracy of the language you use and your pronunciation.

Role play

- Make sure you can ask as well as answer questions.
- Learn the useful phrases which are transferable across the topics, e.g. can I, have you got, where is, I would like, I need, etc.
- Your exam guide is a useful revision tool with key vocabulary and phrases for each topic.
- Prepare as many past role plays as possible.

Presentation

- Choose a topic which interests you which you want to talk about. Keep to a specific topic. Don't be tempted to include something about everything!
- Script your presentation which should last for one and a half minutes. Start by saying what you're going to talk about.
- Remember to include a range of tenses, opinions and descriptions.
- Ask your teacher to correct it.
- Your teacher will give you some questions on your presentation. Prepare your answers to these and get them marked.

- Give a copy of your presentation to your teacher.
- You now need to learn your presentation so that, with the help of five short prompts, you can say it in the exam.
- Some students find it helpful to make a recording of their presentation or to ask their teacher or assistant to do the same to help with pronunciation.

General conversation

- Practise the questions on all the topics for the general conversation with a friend. In your exam your teacher will discuss two or three topics.
- Bring in a cassette for your teacher to make a recording of the questions for you. Listen to them at home.
- Attend the extra sessions which are on offer, with your teacher and with the assistant.
- Listen carefully to the questions.
- Don't forget that you will probably need to change the verb in your answer from the 'you' form to the 'I' or 'we' form in your answer. This isn't always necessary, as with 'there is/there are' questions and answers, for example.
- Remember to say as much as you can. Provide extra detail. Practise saying three or four things in reply to each question if you can.
- Recognise the past/future tense questions and reply with the same tense.
- Give opinions and reasons where possible.

Source: Tile Hill Wood School and Language College

Assessing Attainment Target 3: reading & responding

Assessment of reading can range from comprehension of items of vocabulary in signs, notices, and short messages to longer items in letters, articles, for wider meaning or for guessing meaning from context. Teachers today have access to a wide range of materials, especially with the ability to use authentic Web-based materials, and tend to use the target language in testing language skills even at KS3 as a practice for GCSE. Reading comprehension can be tested through a wide range of activities:

- multiple choice testing of vocabulary/phrases/structures;
- true/false answers;
- matching items (for example words or phrases to symbols, diagrams or pictures, or words to definitions);
- sentence completion;
- using written text to carry out instructions (for example, a recipe, drawing something, creating an object such as a fortune teller or following a route on a map);
- filling gaps with the correct grammatical item or appropriate word or phrase;
- note taking;

Assessment across the age range and across the Attainment Targets

- answering comprehension questions;
- reading a text and identifying or showing understanding of specific words or gist;
- sequencing and re-assembling texts and summaries.

Whatever type is chosen some basic principles remain for test design:

- test only what has been taught;
- test types should match learning activities and tasks;
- the instructions need to be clear and, if in the target language, pitched at the right level;
- diagrams or illustrations used to cue responses must be unequivocal;
- there must be balance between **closed** and **open** activities.

In many cases reading may be combined with other skills so that reading becomes a stimulus for writing, or reading a message may become a cue for speaking on the phone.

Reading for pleasure could be informally assessed by pupils' own evaluations of what they have read in a reading record.

Factors to consider when assessing AT3

- Pronunciation.
- Silent reading for comprehension.
- What sort of reading is required: scanning/skimming/intensive/extensive/detail/gist.
- Reading as a grammatical gap-fill exercise.
- Ability to recognise word formation: cognates, prefixes/suffixes, compound nouns.
- Variety of comprehension: literal (simple retrieval of information from the text); inferential (reading between the lines); reorganisational (combining information from different areas of the text, e.g. summary).
- Amount of support available.
- Opportunities for differentiation.
- Opportunities to provide 'content' or knowledge, cultural knowledge and awareness.

Assessing Attainment Target 4: writing

My homework in modern languages is …

- *good for practising writing skills.* (Boy, 14)

In spite of the equal weighting of the skills, it is often writing which is assessed most regularly, as lessons can be used more productively for speaking and listening tasks and writing lends itself easily to homework. Written tasks for assessment can equally echo the wide range of tasks used generally for class and homework. At a simple level this might include copying items of vocabulary, for example categorising a list of sporting activities into likes/dislikes, indoor/outdoor, summer/winter, etc. Other simple word tasks might include creating anagrams, crosswords or wordsearches, writing words in the correct order or rearranging a text in the correct order. At a higher level pupils could, for example, match captions or speech bubbles to pictures, including gap-filling, sequencing, and then create their own text. Other standard writing tasks which could be used for assessment purposes include sentence or paragraph completion, form-filling, lists, messages, postcards, informal/formal letters, accounts, writing out the results of a survey, adding detail to a written text, writing from picture stimuli

Assessment across the age range and across the Attainment Targets

(photographs/cartoons/a picture series) or getting pupils to research or present a particular topic. Giving the writing task a creative or imaginative slant can at the same time make it more interesting and motivating.

Writing frames or models are particularly helpful in providing pupils with examples and guidance for writing, and in helping pupils to develop their writing. Supporting writing development in this way can equally be used in an assessment task where the structure of the answer is provided or hints are provided on what to include in each section. These could be differentiated so that some pupils receive more support in their writing frame than others.

Factors to consider when assessing AT4

- Presentation of work.
- Accuracy versus spontaneity – marks for content/grammar.
- Classification of error and correction of work by pupils after marking.
- Indication of errors (see, for example, correction symbols in marking policy in Appendix 3).
- Drafting and redrafting to encourage accuracy and use of range of language.
- Is a writing frame or model provided or is it an open-ended task?
- Are reference materials allowed?

In assessing written tasks there are a number of issues to consider relating to accuracy versus spontaneity. While communication of the message remains the most important objective, other factors relating to quality, fluency, range and appropriateness of the language are equally important. The degree of accuracy required may depend on the purpose of the written task: accuracy of form, style and language are clearly vital where a letter is the designated assignment, whereas accuracy may be less crucial in, for example, a note-taking task.

Written assignments need to reflect appropriately work covered in the unit or module, allowing pupils to provide evidence of their achievement in a number of areas. This assessment strategy allows students of different abilities to demonstrate clearly their areas of strength as well as weakness, and enables them to identify areas they need to focus on in order to improve.

At GCSE many schools choose the coursework option rather than the writing exam. Coursework means that good performance is less reliant on memory, pieces for submission can be selected from the best and there is some flexibility in tailoring tasks to pupils' interests. Sharing the marking criteria with pupils and giving them the task of 'marking' a piece of coursework themselves can lead to a better understanding of what is required by close scrutiny of the criteria and the language marked.

Key points	<ul><li>Being totally familiar with the assessment criteria is crucial for accurate assessment.</li><li>At KS3 work is characterised according to the NC level descriptions in each Attainment Target and there is a statutory requirement to report pupils' levels at the end of KS3; at KS4 GCSE criteria apply.</li><li>Making assessment criteria transparent to pupils along with pupil-friendly level and grade descriptions will help pupils to be aware of different levels and grades and what they need to do to improve in order to raise their achievement.</li><li>It is essential to assess all four Attainment Targets to build up a clear picture of a pupil's progress in each skill.</li></ul>

6

Accountability, using assessment data and reporting to parents

The assessment activities, policies and practices described in the previous chapters of this book have been primarily focussed on assessment to help pupils learn; for example by providing feedback and monitoring progress. Records of pupils' progress will of course inform pupils and teachers, but also other potential audiences for assessment information as outlined in Chapter 3.

This chapter considers how some of those audiences can best be kept informed. This includes, for example, advice for report writing and parents' meetings. Also presented are suggestions for using assessment data to set targets (much of which is the type of data resulting from recording outlined in Chapter 3) and improve achievement on an individual and departmental level (for day-to-day pupil targets, see Chapter 4). The chapter also considers some of the issues involved in providing information to outside audiences.

Providing information to outside audiences

It is very unlikely that any parent or Head Teacher will wish to see every mark you have ever recorded for a pupil. But you **will** need to be able to provide information for various people, and this will need to be in an appropriate format for each audience. For example, the Head of Department will need to report to his or her line manager to explain issues such as whether departmental targets have been achieved, as well as identify areas for improvement. Without a starting point and relevant information and records, these areas are very difficult to explain. Each member of the department needs to be able to contribute appropriate information when requested. The HoD will also use information such as this to monitor staff and their performance and individual teachers will need to collate evidence, for example for self-evaluation, performance management meetings, applications for promotion, etc.

 *Assessment is perceived as a nightmare by many staff, though when used accurately it is a reliable tool to help students make progress and achieve their full potential in subjects. It's a short word which involves a huge amount of work, albeit necessary.* (Experienced MFL teacher)

An alternative perspective

A pause for thought ...

For MFL teachers, it can sometimes be an advantage to look at assessment issues from a new perspective, as the world of teaching and Modern Foreign Languages is perhaps sometimes a little too familiar. Looking at the situation in a different context can help to illustrate some fundamental issues.

Ask yourself: How quickly could **you** run 100 metres?

Whatever your answer, it is highly unlikely to be less than ten or eleven seconds: a time such as this would be absolutely world class. To have eleven seconds as your target for the 100 metres would certainly be unrealistic and very probably extremely de-motivating. You would quite likely say to yourself 'I'll never go that quickly! I might as well give up'. A top class male athlete would however find a target of eleven seconds insulting, perhaps, or become complacent that he would achieve the target without trying particularly hard.

Without relevant data on which to base the targets, the process is arbitrary and subjective. Having run a few races and recorded and reflected on the results, appropriate targets become easier to define: the successful athlete has a target of 10.41, I have a target of 23 seconds. **Both** targets are fair, both are (hopefully!) achievable. They are worked out from the prior achievements and predicted improvement with training and practice. An end-of-season report on me, explaining crudely that I had achieved 27 seconds would be almost meaningless without knowing what my potential should have been. A reasoned target gives any information more of a context for the reader of reports and other material. It also gives me as the learner a useful goal: without this, my achievement of 27 seconds might have left me quite content or even complacent, especially if my best friend only did it in 30, so I'd 'beaten' her.

Reflection Task

13

What does assessment mean?

Think of parallels with MFL from the scenario above. What do any marks, reports or grades **mean** to the various audiences? What purpose do they serve?

Using assessment data

Schools now have access to a great deal of data: this data can be used very effectively to predict, monitor and improve achievement, if used alongside helpful formative feedback.

All maintained schools, including maintained special schools, are required to set and publish targets relating to pupil performance in public examinations at the end of KS4 in their governors' annual report to parents. Target setting is used to fit into a cycle of school improvement which involves five stages: analysing current performance, comparing results with similar schools, target setting, action planning and action itself. Targets should be SMART: specific, measurable, achievable, realistic and time-related, and should reflect and reinforce priorities in the school development plan. (See **www.standards. dfee.gov.uk/performance**.) Targets set by schools have to be agreed with the LEA which needs to meet targets set by the government. Once the actual results are published, schools must publish them against their original targets. As there is a direct correlation between prior attainment at the start of a Key Stage and the outcome a pupil achieves, schools may gather a range of data to provide indicators of future attainment.

The following website is used by virtually all schools: **www.standards.dfes.gov.uk/performance**. The main information available there is the **Autumn package** data produced jointly by OFSTED and QCA. It contains **National summary results**, **value-added information** and **Benchmark information**.

This allows schools to:

- understand what progress they are making;
- compare the progress made by individual pupils with progress made by other pupils with similar prior attainment;
- compare their performance with similar schools.

The information guides predictions in both core and non-core subjects, and indicates the minimum predicted target for a pupil with a specific level of prior attainment (i.e. if learners continue to progress at the same rate as they have up to now – the target implies no 'value-added').

To help them make predictions, set targets and measure progress, many schools use some or all of the following:

- the graphs contained in the Autumn package mentioned above, giving national data – average points scores are calculated from statutory assessment tests (SATs) levels and used as an indicator of potential progress, providing a minimum target level for the **average child** in the **average school**; there is no yardstick for foundation subjects such as MFL, but an average score should provide a minimum target;
- data received from such information systems as MIDYIS (Middle Years Information System), YELLIS (Year Eleven Information System) or CATS (Cognitive Ability Test Scores) (depending on what the school has subscribed to): an indication of the pupils' latent ability compared to the national cross-referenced data. It will predict the likely attainment of a pupil in KS3 tests and KS4 common subjects and provides a profile showing strengths and weaknesses in vocabulary, Maths, non-verbal and other skills;
- the school's own information: local data, e.g. performance of the year groups over the last five years; past results compared to the KS3 starting point to show what **this** school can do).

Information from sources such as those listed here can be used to look at specific groups, particularly gender (see further suggestions on p115).

In using assessment data in this way, it is crucial that it is a whole-school initiative for it to function fully. However, principles used in this process can be applied at departmental level, whatever system is employed in the whole school.

To find out what the school 'added value' is, the prediction (e.g. potential GCSE grade) is subtracted from the outcome (e.g. the actual GCSE result). It is this type of data which can be very powerful for:

- determining how realistic predicted grades have been;
- individual teachers' annual reviews of performance;
- departmental reports;
- providing helpful information at parents' evenings (see below, p121).

Schools are consequently involved in making use of a range of data to make accurate judgements of pupils' future potential performance, but data is only useful if it is put into active use and impacts in the classroom. Being informed of previous levels of attainment helps teachers to be aware of the abilities and needs of individual pupils. Setting high, but realistic targets can benefit everyone. However, target setting is not just about furnishing LEA and national statistics; more importantly, target setting is a genuine way of stretching pupils to achieve realistic objectives.

Collecting data to track progress from school assessments needs to be limited to valid, reliable data from tests undertaken in 'exam' conditions. In MFL this should ideally comprise all four skills at least twice a year, and should include a rigorous moderation procedure to ensure that the data produced is reliable and valid. Teachers' own records of evidence are vital components here if the test results do not, in the teacher's judgement, reflect the attainment of the pupil.

Trainee/NQT Task

Target setting in school

Find out how your schools are tackling the issue of target setting.

- What data do they use?
- Do they make use of national and local statistics?
- How is this information adapted into targets?
- How are targets monitored?

Using data in this sort of way can sometimes appear overwhelming and very abstract, especially if the process is new to you. Yet it can also be very heartening to find that your pupils are achieving at or above their predicted minimum targets, or that your lower ability group achieved in a key task identified by the department (see Chapter 3) slightly better as a group than last year's did. The message is clear: if using the data helps raise pupils' achievement and their confidence and motivation, it is worth doing.

Assessment is gathering data to use as a tool to inform future teaching, planning and learning targets, and communicate with others. (Experienced MFL teacher)

A word of caution: Weeden et al (2002: 128) warn us that we should be wary of labelling pupils with data and predictions. We would certainly agree that it is dangerous to categorise pupils and limit their potential. However, if employed in a positive way to help improvement and to help pupils see their true potential, the process is to be encouraged.

Important points

- National data can help provide predictions, but so can departmental data kept from year to year (e.g. from key tests).
- National data helps schools compare like with like – there is not very much to be gained from comparing two very different types of school.
- Collecting and analysing the data is only going to improve learning if something is done with the information.

Accountability, using assessment data and reporting to parents

Possible areas for departmental focus

Using assessment data, whether school or departmentally based, the department could focus on one or more of the following groups or comparisons, according to need:

- gender;
- specific foreign language;
- achievement of dual linguists;
- achievements in key assessment tasks for different ability sets;
- Year 7 results from various feeder primaries;
- birth dates;
- pupils starting at different NC levels;
- pupils with EAL;
- actual against predicted GCSE grades;
- LEA averages.

OFSTED has produced some very clear questions to be asked by a Head of Department about using assessment data:

> *As heads of department, working with subject teachers, do we:*
>
> - *analyse carefully pupils' current standards and how well different groups are doing?*
>
> - *make sure we have enough evidence to evaluate learning? Do we include the views and responses of pupils, lesson observation by a variety of people, the quality of work produced by pupils and their assessed progress in each component or Attainment Target of the subject?*
>
> - *have high, clear expectations for the regular assessment of pupils' progress and the feedback we give to them and their parents? Do we assure the quality and accuracy of marking and assessment by monitoring, moderation and, where necessary, intervention?*
>
> - *maintain clear, simple records on pupils' progress (including statutory ones for pupils with special educational needs)? Do we store completed work and assessments, where appropriate using ICT, and avoid duplication of effort or unnecessary bureaucracy?*
>
> - *liaise effectively with partner schools and post-16 institutions over the curriculum and the transfer of assessment information? Do we aim to ensure that pupils' progress between phases and key stages is smooth and uninterrupted?*
>
> (OFSTED 2002a)

Target setting

Chapter 4 contained ideas for setting learning targets for pupils when giving feedback and responding to their work. Motivation can be improved by setting achievable targets based on available reliable data. This enables teachers to predict what learners are likely to achieve, or, perhaps better, what they are **capable** of achieving. Teachers do not need to be statisticians in order to do this!

Any targets are individual to **them** as learners – pupils are not competing with anyone else. This enables much clearer statements to be made about pupils' achievement and progress: true, this particular learner is not going to achieve an A grade, but their D is one grade better than the predicted attainment.

Accountability, using assessment data and reporting to parents

In most schools, form tutors will develop an overview of how an individual pupil is progressing; they will build this rounded picture from the reports obtained from subject teachers at the designated times of the year, as well as from, for example, information on rewards and sanctions issued by various teachers. The form tutor will usually work with an individual pupil to set overall targets for their learning and progress generally, but it is with the subject teacher that these targets will need to be refined to be applicable at the subject level.

In order for target setting and use of data to be successful, there must be collaboration and communication between staff in the same department and school, as well as between institutions. Assessment information has to be understandable by all, and has to be passed on.

The European Language Portfolio

One way to ensure records are transferred between institutions and situations and that records are used and considered is to adopt a common, recognised approach. A starting point might be the European Language Portfolio (ELP), which is linked to part of the Common European Framework.

Alan Dobson (2000: 204) has described the European Language Portfolio as follows:

> *The ELP is a means of assessment which enables learners to keep a recognised record of all their language learning achievements both in formal education and training and outside these contexts. It comprises three parts:*
> * *a 'passport' recording formal qualifications;*
> * *a language biography, describing in more detail both knowledge of specific languages and learning experiences such as visits and exchanges or work experience abroad;*
> * *and a language dossier in which the learner may include samples of work or other evidence to support and illustrate the language biography.*
>
> *It follows that the ELP should be progressively updated by learners as their language learning develops and career transition points are reached, such as changing school or applying for a job.*

Parallels can be drawn here with pupil Records of Achievement, and with the professional portfolios which are developed by trainee teachers and are now being continued throughout a teaching career to illustrate achievements and provide evidence for threshold and other applications.

Comprehensive information about the portfolio can be found at **http://culture2. coe.int/portfolio**. CILT has already developed Portfolios for junior and adult learners (**www.cilt.org.uk**).

Targets for pupils/teaching groups

There is, as we have maintained throughout this book, no point having targets if they are not monitored and if the pupils are not reminded of them. The targets could be incorporated into plenary activities in some lessons, in addition to looking at normal lesson objectives. Reflecting on these targets, both day-to-day ones and longer term, can help identify learning difficulties and queries, but also can emphasise successes and (even small) steps forward.

Class discussion on possible targets can be part of these plenary sessions; taking perhaps only five minutes of the lesson. This short period of time can result in some very useful ideas for improvements in teaching and learning – it is certainly a worthwhile investment. The ideal is to have pupils devising their own or group targets, but this process is best started initially by the teacher suggesting some realistic possibilities.

Choosing a class target

It is crucial to choose something to track or measure that is worth measuring and which will benefit you and the pupils. It needs to be worth the effort and it must be clear enough for all to see what is being measured, why, and how it can be improved. If you can choose a target to start with that you are fairly certain can be met but which the class nevertheless has to work at, this should set the positive tone needed.

Visual representation

In order for the target and progress to be clear to everyone, a visual representation is helpful. This should, of course, be done where possible without naming individuals. This could be something as simple as total vocabulary points gained by the class each week (see the example graph below), where some of the vocabulary learning strategies from Chapter 3 are used, and improvements tracked.

In a class of 30 Year 7 pupils, the target agreed with the class is 280 points from vocabulary tests (where each test is out of ten). The class has been doing well, but the teacher knows they can achieve more. The vocabulary tests comprise language with which they should be very familiar and she wishes to promote excellence. If and when the class achieve the target consistently over a number of weeks, it may be appropriate to raise the goal.

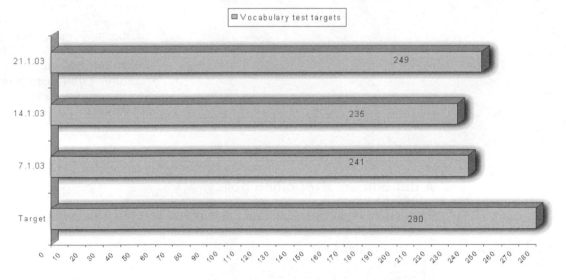

● 10	**Class targets**
Departmental Task	Look at the example of the visual representation of a class target above.
	• Discuss as a department which classes in particular may benefit from this approach.
	• How could you reward and publicise achievement of class targets such as this?

Accountability, using assessment data and reporting to parents

Reports and report writing

Information contained in a report

Reports vary considerably from school to school, reflecting different contexts. But there are certain features which should appear in any report.

A report should always be:

■ professionally presented;
■ understandable by various readers (the mark scheme must be explained – if effort is marked A–D for example, it might be right to assume D is less than A, but how do we know that with grades 1–4?);
■ reasonably concise.

The lists below contain the types of information found in a range of MFL reports.

STANDARD DETAILS	GRADES/MARKS/FIGURES	COMMENTS
• name of learner; • year group; • subject; • date/year; • form/tutor group; • summary of course content (main points from scheme of work: themes and language); • space for parental/guardian signature/comment (often on the overall report).	These should come with an explanatory key for: • achievement; • effort; • organisation; • homework; • tests; • attendance/punctuality; • mock exam results/coursework; • KS3 NC AT levels achieved; • merits/commendations; • detentions.	Prose style comments in many reports, but also ticks after certain phrases: • how the pupil is progressing against his or her targets; • how the pupil is learning/participating in class; • how the pupil is behaving in class; • what the pupil needs to do in order to improve (specific targets); • other comments on pupil's activities, attitude, etc (e.g. a particularly impressive piece of work or extra involvement in language clubs etc); • comment from pupil/student on their progress and future intentions.

A departmental reporting policy

The extract below is taken from the departmental reporting policy at Coundon Court School, Coventry, an 11–18 mixed comprehensive school, and is written by Maria Cutler, HoD.

Accountability, using assessment data and reporting to parents

Departmental reporting policy

A report is any written communication about a pupil's experience and achievement to parents or others with a legitimate interest.

The purpose of reporting is to provide information about a pupil's progress, attainment and achievement in relation to the school curriculum, to parents and others who need to know.

The principles of reporting are that:

- results of assessment should be presented in a positive manner, indicating what the pupil has achieved and pointing to what needs to be done;

- reports about pupils' progress should ensure that attainment in National Curriculum assessments are set into the context of pupils' achievements and experiences;

- the school should provide opportunities for teacher-pupil dialogue so that pupils clearly understand and share learning and assessment objectives;

- there should be a coherent approach to writing reports;

- reports should not merely be descriptive but evaluative and written in context to include illuminative comments.

Reports should aim to cover:

- general progress in the language;

- attitude and motivation;

- performance and achievement in each of the four skills of listening, speaking, reading and writing;

- homework and learning;

- future targets.

Useful information when writing reports:

- They should be completed in black/blue ink.

- The full name of the pupil should head the report (though their usual name may be referred to in the comment (e.g. Samantha/Sam).

- Reports must be handed to the Head of Department in advance of the deadline date for checking before they are passed on to the form tutor.

- At KS4/5 pupils write their own comment. It may be useful to discuss suggestions with individual pupils before they complete it.

Source: Coundon Court School

My strongest point is listening, but I still need more practice, so I plan to go to the language lab on Tuesday lunchtimes to practise listening. My weakest point is reading. I find reading Spanish quite hard and I could practise this by doing some of the reading exercises we have been given. (Year 11 pupil: comment on report)

  14

Reflection Task

Reports

Look at reports in your school and department. Ask yourself:

- If I were an outsider, what exactly would this report tell me?

- What information does it contain from the list above?

- Is there a case for including any of the information not incorporated at the moment?

- Do they need to be made more comprehensible?

- Who do you think would benefit from the report and how? (Parent, learner, teacher ...)

- Are the categories self-explanatory/helpful?

- How do they change with the age of the pupil?

- What records would you need to have in order to be able to complete these reports effectively?

Helping teachers complete useful and consistent reports

It is still the case that some reports are issued with a few ticks and a bland comment such as 'fine', or 'doing well', or even the old favourite 'could do better'. This is to some extent perfectly understandable: many staff are very pressured with the number of pupils for whom they have to produce reports. However, it may also be a case of a teacher having insufficient knowledge, or inadequate records. It is also worth considering how informative such a report might be for a parent or a pupil. It probably wouldn't help either of them very much and, it could be argued, would not be worth the minimal effort expended to produce it.

Many Heads of Department produce a **bank of report comments.** Using ICT, these are then easily incorporated into reports and adapted and personalised as necessary. Reports can also include targets, a selection of which can be found in INSET/ITE Task 8, p136.

The advantages of a system such as this include:

- the HoD knows that all staff, whatever their experience, will be able to use informative comments;
- it can save teachers time;
- it enables teachers to comment on a range of issues;
- it means staff are not recycling the same, perhaps idiosyncratic, turn of phrase again and again (provided they vary their choice from the bank);
- where ICT is used, comments on pupils can be retained and used to help inform targets and feedback as the term/year progresses;
- if the bank of comments is stored electronically and available centrally to all members of the department, it can be added to as appropriate: all staff, whatever their experience can contribute. It is not therefore an imposition from above, and a true example of sharing good practice;
- not least, it helps iron out spelling and typographical errors: in schools where staff write comments on a communal page, everybody has to rewrite their comments where one person has made a mistake!

One main challenge with report writing is meeting deadlines smoothly. The HoD can be a great help here, particularly for newly qualified teachers. Deadlines for reports obviously need to be highlighted prior to the start of the academic year. In addition to this, reports can be a standing item on the departmental meeting agenda, marks for key pieces of work can be recorded as they are collected onto electronic versions of reports; comments on particular achievements of individual pupils can be entered onto electronic versions of reports as they happen. This last point is particularly true of informal assessment of speaking activities, for example (see Chapter 5). As with any big task, the challenge becomes less stressful when broken down into achievable 'chunks'. HoDs can also ask to see a selection of reports from an NQT (and other staff as deemed appropriate) to avoid dozens being submitted incomplete or erroneously.

We would add here that your record keeping and therefore your mark book is of crucial help when writing reports. Effective record keeping will make report writing much easier, more accurate and of greater benefit to your pupils.

Parents are entitled to see their child's school records, although this does not necessarily include teachers' individual mark books. But these are invaluable for writing reports and elucidating your comments at parents' evenings.

Parents' meetings and other contacts

Meetings with parents or carers offer an excellent opportunity to share information on the pupil and their learning, and to pinpoint ways forward. It is, of course, not always the case that the parents to whom you wish to talk are present at official parents' evenings. Other ways of sharing the information (e.g. reports, letters home) are therefore vital.

What information do parents require?

A raw number or grade may be one element parents want, but they are of course interested in how their children are in class, real-life examples of what they have done, comments on the homework they know took their child three hours to do. Try to say something positive about all your pupils – and have concrete, understandable advice and targets. It is much more effective if you can show what was expected/predicted for the pupil and how this has been matched/surpassed/underachieved. Keeping good records is essential here and can be re-used in reports.

Marianne Tchakhotine, French teacher at Henley in Arden High School, recommends using clear, visual graphs of particular Year 10 and 11 students' achievements at parents' evening.

When I was able to show parents exactly how their daughter or son had performed in their mock exams in each skill, we had a much more useful conversation, where they were asking about how they could help their child practise speaking or writing in French for example. I demonstrated with a bar chart how the mock results compared with their predicted grade. It has resulted in a very detailed plan of how the Year 11 students will prepare and check their progress in the next few months.

Parents' evening checklist

The following advice will not be necessary for experienced teachers, but trainee teachers and NQTs may find it useful.

Personal preparation/presentation

- A professional, smart appearance is vital – take something to school to change into if you're not going home in between.
- Have everything at hand – appointments sheet, watch, records, etc.
- Try to sit in a comfortable chair at a decent-sized table or desk.
- Shake hands, smile, look confident.
- Have a name card on your desk and introduce yourself.
- Have an emergency plan if things go wrong, especially if you are an NQT – perhaps to alert HoD or senior teacher.
- Keep to time, and try to finish each appointment as positively as possible.

Accountability, using assessment data and reporting to parents

Professional preparation

- Ensure you know the correct surname – not always the same as the pupil's.
- If there is something you are concerned about, this is the chance to ask about it – but if it is something very serious, the parent should have been alerted by you, perhaps through the year head or form tutor already.
- You need to think about how you will express your comments if the pupil is there (this is increasingly common now).
- All relevant records need to be up-to-date and available.
- Consider extracting the main information and presenting it professionally in a folder: readable, well-presented records give a very good impression to the parents, and are less likely to be misread by you.
- Arrange your pile of work/folders/exercise books in alphabetical or appointment order to find as easily as possible.
- Work out what you will say about each pupil – both positive and constructive comments.
- Targets and ways forward should form the main part of the conversation rather than criticism.
- Make sure you cover everything needed in the time allotted – but give parents time to talk/react/ask too.
- Ethics – it should not be possible for parents to read information or grades on any other pupils in your class.

Other parental contact

This usually only arises when there's a problem, but it is becoming more common to alert parents when there is something positive to report. Secondary schools do not tend to do this as often as primary schools (or it's not as apparent). At primary level, for example, it is normal for pupils to come home with stickers on their jumpers – in secondary they're hidden in their exercise books if at all; in primary, pieces of work are clutched in hands or emptied by parents from bags – not usually the case at secondary. It may be worth considering how individual achievements can be communicated to parents.

 21

Trainee/NQT Task

Parents' evening role play

During your block placements, ask your subject mentor to pick any pupil from any of your classes and 'act' as his or her mother or father. You should be able to respond to your mentor's questions and give him or her relevant information using your records and personal knowledge of the pupil. Your mentor could ask about progress, behaviour, particular language skills, what the pupil could do to improve, etc (an expanded version of this task is on p134, INSET/ITE Task 6). This is especially useful for preparing yourself for dealing with difficult questions.

4

Head of Department Task

Parents' evenings

- Produce a checklist for parents' evenings of material members of staff should have available for reference, based on the information on pp121–122 and your school's usual practice.

- Consider pairing up more and less experienced members of staff. This can be very reassuring and any queries can be dealt with quickly.

- If you have trainee teachers in your department, arrange for them to shadow you or their mentor for a parents' evening. Give them a specific task, e.g. to identify ways you explain achievement to parents of pupils with a range of different abilities.

 *Assessment is providing information for you the teacher, for the pupil and for the parents.* (Experienced MFL teacher)

 5

Head of Department Task

Assessment expectations

Look at the expectations below from experienced MFL subject mentors.

- What expectations regarding assessment and marking practices would you have of:
  a) trainee teachers;
  b) NQTs;
  c) experienced members of staff?

- How would they differ?

> *I expect trainee teachers to ...*
> - *assess students informally in class – use school record book.*
> - *assess formally – Y7–10 exams.*
> - *write Y7 reports and attend parents' evening – therefore assessment is important.*
> - *look at target setting/support with Y11 on this.*
> (MFL subject mentor)
>
> *I expect trainee teachers to ...*
> - *be capable of accurate marking.*
> - *to have knowledge of the NC levels/school requirements.*
> - *to be capable of analysing the school data with input from the school's Assessment Manager.*
> - *to be capable of presenting parents with prescriptive analyses.*
> (MFL subject mentor)

Key points

- Assessment information needs to be communicated effectively to a range of audiences, including parents.

- Assessment data can be used positively to improve achievement and raise motivation.

- With careful consideration and planning, this use of assessment information can be of benefit to pupils, teachers and outside audiences.

Accountability, using assessment data and reporting to parents

7

Suggestions for pre-service and in-service training activities

The activities in this chapter can be adapted for use within a department or in a training session, perhaps for pre-service teachers or NQTs. Some of them aim at practising specific assessment techniques in MFL teaching and learning, or at producing concrete outcomes for the department. Others are intended to get participants thinking about what assessment is all about. A number of other ideas for departmental activities are to be found in the previous chapters of this book (see contents).

We will take you through each stage of the activity, indicating who might find it most useful, how long it will need and any preparation needed.

The activities in this chapter are as follows:

- INSET/ITE Task 1: What are assessment criteria?
- INSET/ITE Task 2: Successful test design
- INSET/ITE Task 3: Departmental assessment 'stock take'
- INSET/ITE Task 4: Self evaluation
- INSET/ITE Task 5: Learning about assessing pupils
- INSET/ITE Task 6: Parent's evening role play
- INSET/ITE Task 7: Marking appropriately
- INSET/ITE Task 8: Target setting

INSET/ITE
Task

What are assessment criteria?

Suitable for	Trainees/NQTs.
Objective	To highlight some fundamental principles involved in assessment. This task is also useful as an ice-breaker, to stimulate discussion about assessment.
Preparation	– The instructions on Web template 7 (see p126) should be copied on to OHP transparency. – Participants need to be divided into three fairly equal groups. – Each group needs a blank OHP transparency and an OHP pen.
Time required	Approximately one hour in total (introduction, approximately fifteen minutes group discussion, followed by presentations and conclusions).

Task

Each group has to prepare assessment criteria for one of three 'competitions':
a) cake competition;
b) pop idol contest;
c) best comedy sketch on TV in one year.

NB: all three tasks are challenging, but Task a) is the most straightforward and Task c) the most demanding. You may wish to take this into account when allocating tasks to groups.

Introduction: look at the Introduction to this book (pp1–6).

During the task

You may need to suggest some possible criteria/categories to groups, depending how the discussions are progressing. Some possibilities might be as follows:

a) Cake: criteria – taste (does it make your mouth water?); presentation (is it uniformly shaped?); originality (does it show independent thought?); ease of handling, texture, aroma; what rules might be necessary – type of cake, time limit, same equipment, same ingredients, cost.

b) Pop idol: criteria (see also table below) – stage presence (confidence, extrovert, *je ne sais quoi,* charismatic, relates to audience, dance skills); singing (style, tone, range, unique qualities); personality (fashionable, committed, sense of humour, open-minded); problems – defining such things as 'the x factor'; what rules might be necessary – age of contestant, type of song.

c) Comedy sketch: criteria – 'laughability' (laughter Richter scale)/appeal across age, gender/lack of offensive material/financially viable/originality/viewing figures/visual humour/linguistic humour; problems – humour is very subjective; possible rules – must be original, must be between one and three minutes long.

If groups' results do not yield sufficient material, the Assessment criteria table overleaf can be presented to participants after they have had their group discussions and made their presentations. It relates only to task **b)**, but can be used to stimulate discussion, along with the suggestions for each task above.

• What do the criteria mean?

• How would you know someone met the criteria (or not)?

• How do you decide if a 'performance' fits a particular category?

Links are clearly apparent here with National Curriculum level descriptors and assessment grids used in various external examinations and coursework – the key is to make them transparent and useable.

Assessment criteria	<<<<< Levels >>>>>		
Criteria	'No way'	'Maybe'	'Brilliant'
Voice	Can't hold a note	Misses odd note (karaoke style)	Excellent pitch and tone
Musical talent	No talent	Can deliver a song	Makes song their own
Looks	Frankly unappealing	Worth a double take	Drop dead gorgeous
Personality	Wet fish	Can hold a conversation	Witty and sparkly
X factor	X-Files	X-pected	X-traordinary
Age	Over the hill	On top of the hill	Approaching base camp

Discussion

Some of the most important issues to highlight are:

- learners (or in the case of these competitions, contestants) needing to know **what** they are being judged on;
- objectivity/transparency of assessment criteria;
- difficulty of quantifying or categorising certain qualities;
- balancing categories – in MFL, communication and accuracy for example.

Web template **7**

Instructions for INSET/ITE Task 1

You are judges in one of three competitions.

Your task, as a group, is to design assessment criteria/level descriptors where possible for the competition below allotted to your group:

a) cake competition

b) pop idol contest

c) best comedy sketch on TV in one year

You will need to present your results on an OHT, and describe the ease or difficulty with which you were able to design the criteria.

You have 15 minutes.

Suggestions for pre-service and in-service training activities

2

**INSET/ITE
Task**

Successful test design

Objectives	– To consider how effective a published end-of-unit/topic test is.
	– To produce an end-of-unit/topic test based on specific criteria, perhaps adapted from the original.

Preparation	– You will need a copy of an end-of-unit test for each language in the department (it does not need to be a test you have used and if you think the test is not particularly suitable for your context, then that could be very productive in this activity).
	– Participants need to work in language-specific groups.

Time required	Two hours – work in groups (one hour per task) plus preparation time.

Task A

Using an end-of-unit test from the current coursebook/scheme of work, analyse the test according to the following questions:
- how clear are the instructions/rubrics?
- how well set out is the test?
- which skills are being tested (listening/speaking/reading/writing)?
- what is the **balance** of skills (e.g. how much TL reading is expected when testing listening etc)?
- what kind of language **exactly** is being tested (vocabulary, grammatical structures, idioms …)?
- what **types** of tasks are expected (e.g. multi-choice, gap fill, open-ended questions, re-ordering of sentences, true/false, matching pairs, etc)?
- what **stimulus language** is used (e.g. 'authentic' language, advertisements, letters etc.)?
- how are marks allocated?

Then consider these wider questions:
- how clear are the assessment criteria, i.e. would two teachers come to the same conclusion?
- what would the results of this test tell you about learners' progress?
- what feedback could you usefully give: **a)** individuals, **b)** the whole group, about the test?
- how could you best prepare learners for similar tests?
- does it actually test what it sets out to test?
- what does it **not** assess?

Report back on these questions to the other groups.

Task B

Design a short test for a group of pupils.

- What do you want to know about the pupils' learning (e.g. gist comprehension, manipulation of a structure, recognition of vocabulary …)?
- What activities will best show what they have learned?
- What will be your assessment criteria?
- Will your chosen test(s) actually test what you want it to?
- How will you ensure that the layout and instructions enable ease of completion and access to the task?
- Will your test enable all pupils to show what they know?
- Will you differentiate within the test/will you include progression throughout the test?
- How will you devise your mark scheme?
- What marks will you record and how?

Suggestions for pre-service and in-service training activities

Present your test to the other groups.

Then follow up: what conclusions do you reach in the light of this activity regarding:
• the suitability of the tests you have looked at;
• the implications for other tests you use;
• the practicality (or otherwise) of designing your own tests;
• the possibility of adapting current tests.

3

**INSET/ITE
Task**

Departmental assessment 'stock take'

| Objectives | – To consider what position the department is in with regard to assessment.
– To plan any developments as necessary.

This activity is not intended to look at any specific issue in detail; rather to enable the department to begin the process of development. The results of the meeting could form the basis of an action plan. |

| Preparation | – Make sure that everyone has copies of current school and departmental assessment policies and practices.
– The Head of Department and each member of staff should have looked at a copy of the departmental assessment tables below at least a week before the meeting (see also Web template 8). |

| Time required | Pre-meeting reading approximately one hour, meeting – one hour. |

Task

Look at the following three tables and, as a department, discuss the current situation as it applies to you.

Web template 8

Departmental assessment 'stock take'

Departmental policies and documentation

Assessment issue	In our policy?	Understood/ applied by all staff?	Action needed?	If yes, …		
				What?	By whom?	When?
The departmental schemes of work integrate assessment opportunities						
Key assessment tasks indicated in scheme of work						
The PoS is covered fully in the SoW						
Assessment **for** learning						
Assessment **of** learning						

Departmental practice

Assessment issue	In our policy?	Understood/ applied by all staff?	Action needed?	If yes, ...		
				What?	By whom?	When?
All four skills are assessed regularly						
Reports to parents are clear and informative						
Planning/teaching/ assessment integrated						
Data recorded systematically						
Assessment data used appropriately						
Homework to further learning						
Lesson evaluation pro forma used appropriately						
Peer evaluation of lessons						

Pupil experience

Assessment issue	In our policy?	Understood/ applied by all staff?	Action needed?	If yes, ...		
				What?	By whom?	When?
Written academic guidance to pupils						
Pupils understand learning objectives						
Learning is reviewed at the end of lessons						
Assessment criteria: clear to pupils						
Benchmarks (e.g. model answers) provided						
Target setting: individual pupils						
Target setting: groups/classes						
Constructive, specific feedback						
Pupil self-assessment/review						

Suggestions for pre-service and in-service training activities

INSET/ITE
Task

Self evaluation

Objectives	– To consider an individual teacher's assessment practice and understanding.
	– To begin to plan for individual development.
	– To contribute to departmental development of assessment policies and practice.

| **Preparation** | The following pen portraits of three teachers have been compiled using level descriptors (developed by one higher education institution) which apply to the standards trainee teachers are required to achieve in order to acquire Qualified Teacher Status. As a professional development tool, they are equally applicable to more experienced teachers. Heads of Department should encourage all members of the team to use these as the basis for developing an action plan for professional development. There is a suggestion for an approach for Heads of Department to use with these portraits in Chapter 2 (see p32). |

The descriptions cover a wide range of assessment approaches and practices, including much of the material discussed in this book.

| **Time required** | Will vary depending on individual needs. |

Task

Read through the pen portraits of three different types of teachers.

- For each one, consider how you would evaluate each teacher's practice. What, if anything, would each one need to improve upon?
- Can you recognise yourself in any of the portraits or in elements of each? Undoubtedly you will find it difficult to fit completely into one category – but you should be able to identify various aspects.
- Highlight the areas you feel fairly confident about in one colour, and those you feel you are less confident with in another.
- What elements do you need to work on to develop your own assessment practice?
- How will you go about this?
- What do you need to help you in this process?
- Can you focus on one or two aspects which will help improve your pupils' learning and contribute to evidence of your own professional development?

Teacher A

- Uses a range of strategies to make accurate assessments of pupils' achievements; uses these assessments to inform planning and teaching.
- Lesson plans are cross-referenced with relevant programme of study (PoS), syllabuses and level descriptors, where appropriate.
- Sets suitable objectives for sequences of lessons and plans how they will be assessed.
- Provides opportunities to consolidate classroom learning and sets homework in line with school/departmental policies.
- Produces some evidence of improved teaching through self-evaluation and target-setting over a period of time.
- Is familiar with and understands the basic subject framework (relevant programmes of study, level and end of key stage descriptions).
- Accurate knowledge of section of specification being taught and some awareness of how it fits into the whole.
- Able to evaluate extent to which learning objectives have been achieved and take appropriate action, including where ICT has been used.
- Makes assessment of pupils' understanding during teaching and gives feedback to pupils; encourages pupils to reflect on their own performance.
- Provides constructive oral and written feedback on pupils' work and sets targets based on this.
- Monitors strengths and weaknesses using focused observation, questioning and testing, as appropriate; uses and assesses ICT as appropriate.
- Maintains adequate records of pupils' work and achievements in order to provide evidence of progress and attainment.
- Familiar with statutory and school policy requirements on assessment and reporting to parents.
- Accurate knowledge of relevant assessment requirements and procedures for NC, KS4 and post-16.
- Knows how national, local and school data can be used to set targets for pupils' achievement.
- Appropriate use of routine assessment procedures including NC and other standardised tests.

Teacher B

- Regularly plans informal and structured opportunities to assess pupils' progress.
- Integrates assessment evidence into future planning and teaching.
- Longer term planning is routinely linked with relevant programmes of study.
- Objectives are clearly related to the sequence of lessons and demonstrate an understanding of progression.
- Uses a range of strategies in various settings to consolidate learning, including through homework.
- Regularly engages in developmental cycles of self evaluation, target setting, action. etc to improve teaching.
- More detailed knowledge and understanding of requirements in terms of subject knowledge, relevant programmes of study, level and end of key stage descriptions.
- Understands the links between what is being taught at KS4/post 16 and other parts of the syllabus; familiar with other current syllabuses.
- Recognises the various ways in which pupils demonstrate achievement and makes use of the information.
- Feedback is carefully related to learning objectives; involves pupils in reviewing their own work in order to note strengths as well as areas for improvement.
- More able to recognise the needs of individual pupils and set appropriate targets for them.
- Incorporates explicit evidence of pupils' understanding and progress into planning and teaching through systematic assessment and recording of progress.
- Records are systematic and form an effective basis for setting and reviewing learning objectives and for reporting on pupils' progress.
- Has made a useful contribution to statutory assessment and reporting requirements. Able to interpret and apply NC levels, and KS4/post-16 course requirements consistently.
- Makes occasional use of assessment data to set challenging but realistic targets.
- Uses a range of assessment methods for a variety of purposes.

Teacher C

- Is able to set clear assessment criteria, make effective use of planned opportunities for assessment and use this information explicitly when planning for teaching and learning.
- Able to make a contribution to departmental subject planning.
- Objectives, resources and outcomes are clearly inter-related and an understanding of progression is explicit.
- Helps pupils to recognise the importance of consolidating learning and to accept some responsibility for it.
- Employs self evaluation and target setting with particular skill and insight to improve teaching.
- Routinely demonstrates the ability to link own subject knowledge with the National Curriculum framework.
- Has a command of and confidence with 14–19 syllabuses; some awareness of new developments.
- Responds readily and flexibly to information on pupil achievement.
- Targets feedback effectively to meet individual needs and to challenge and support pupils' understanding; finds ways to engage pupils in evaluating their own work so that their performance is improved.
- Routinely encourages learning by using feedback to negotiate individual targets.
- Systematic assessment and detailed and accurate recording of pupils' progress on a regular basis and at greater depth, gaining insight into individual pupils as well as groups.
- Has taken some responsibility for statutory assessment and reporting requirements.
- Contributes intelligently to departmental discussions and moderation, and to the appraisal of assessment requirements.
- Routinely uses assessment information as an integral part of target setting.
- Makes a critical and intelligent use of assessment showing awareness of the biases and limitations of different procedures.

Suggestions for pre-service and in-service training activities

5

**INSET/ITE
Task**

Learning about assessing pupils

Objectives	– To discover as much as possible about pupils' learning from one assessment task.

– To consider some assessment 'fundamentals'.

– To consider how pupils' learning can effectively be assessed.

– To analyse what can be learned from such assessment.

Preparation	Trainee teachers or NQTs choose at least one task/activity/ homework or test they have carried out with learners (the activity may be appropriate for other teachers too).

Time required	Varied, depending upon assessment task chosen. Time for meeting to discuss outcomes: 30–45 minutes.

Task

Ask the trainee or NQT to provide:
- the mark scheme/marking criteria they devised or used;
- a copy of each pupil's marked response to the task;
- an analysis of what this task told them about: **a)** individuals, **b)** the class, **c)** the task, **d)** the mark scheme;
- a copy of the relevant page from their mark book showing the recording of the marks/information;
- a discussion of how the assessment of learning informed their subsequent planning (for example, a revised version of the task/test/instructions to show **exactly** how they would improve it) and how they intend to build on their progress in assessment;
- a plan of how they can be more effective in their marking and assessment and how they will know.

After the discussion
- Agree on a date for a follow-up meeting to discuss progress.
- If the outcomes are very good, ask the trainee/NQT if they could present their findings at a department meeting or if they could copy them for circulation.

INSET/ITE
Task

Parents' evening role play

People involved	Mentor/HoD and Trainee/NQT.
Objectives	– To help trainees or NQTs prepare for parents' evenings. – To raise trainees' or NQTs' awareness of the importance of effective and useable record-keeping.
Preparation	Ensure trainee or NQT brings their assessment records to a meeting with you.
Time required	Time for meeting to conduct role play and discuss outcomes: 30 minutes approximately.

Task

Select an appropriate class, i.e. one for which the trainee or NQT has responsibility. Choose any pupil's name and play the role of the parent or guardian of that pupil: the trainee or NQT should respond fully and professionally.

Ask the trainee/NQT:
• How is (name) doing?

Expect details of:
• knowledge of pupil as an individual;
• reasonably detailed marks/grades/targets;
• overview of effort/attitude in class and with homework.

Ask the trainee/NQT:
• what can I do to help him/her?

Expect:
• advice on learning strategies/language learning strategies;
• specific advice for the individual – i.e. where strengths and weaknesses are.

If you want to really stretch them, ask a question frequently put by parents:
• but why should (name) learn a foreign language anyway?

Repeat this process with three or four pupils, from different Key Stages where possible.

7

**INSET/ITE
Task**

Marking appropriately

 Objectives
– To discuss a variety of approaches to marking.
– To match marking approaches to a range of learning activities.
– To raise awareness of alternative marking approaches.

Preparation
The text below on Web template 9 should be copied on to OHP transparency.

Time required
45 minutes: 5 minutes introduction, 20 minutes discussion individually or in pairs, 20 minutes discussion as a group.

Web template 9

Appropriate marking

Appropriate marking

When marking: which of the marking approaches 1–15 below is appropriate in various contexts (a–j)?

For each activity, discuss your choices and decide which approach or approaches would be most effective.

Discuss also which approaches, if any, you have not used yourself and whether you would consider doing so.

Your decisions will then be discussed with the other members of the department.

a   a class reading task carried out in pairs

b   a final piece of written project work

c   a multi-choice listening exercise

d   a piece of homework where pupils made notes on a piece of TL they had read

e   a vocabulary test TL to English

f   a vocabulary test English to TL

g   three sentences with gaps to fill in with past participles

h   a paragraph on 'my weekend' based on a model

i   an invented short poem

j   an argumentative piece on the adoption or otherwise of the euro in Britain

1   Tick/cross

2   In pen/pencil/different colour

3   Underline/circle error but don't correct (encouraging the pupil to work it out)

4   Using different colour highlighter pens

5   Grid with overlay on OHT with correct responses

6   Using the 'Insert Comment' feature of a word processing programme

7   Collecting work and giving feedback on it via e-mail

8   Pupils mark own work in a different colour according to an OHT discussed as a class

9   Swap papers

10   Abbreviation/symbols/codes in margin, e.g. spelling, grammar, syntax

11   Comments in English/TL in margin/line in between

12   Comments at end – English/TL – critical/constructive

13   Marks out of, e.g. 10 with/without comment

14   NC level awarded

15   List of corrections to do

8

**INSET/ITE
Task**

Target setting

| Objectives | – To evaluate departmental practice in target setting.
– To reflect on some suggested targets.
– To adapt departmental policy/practice as appropriate. |

| Preparation | Teachers need a copy of both examples of targets in Modern Languages (see below) and your own departmental equivalents if available. |

| Time required | One hour: 15 minutes reading time, 30 minutes paired/ group discussion, 15 minutes plenary discussion. |

Task

Look at the examples of targets from two schools. The two sets of targets are aimed at different audiences. The first is aimed directly at pupils; the second is provided for teachers to select targets as appropriate. The examples depend obviously to some extent on school context, e.g. the availability of a languages open access area, but can be adapted to your situation as appropriate.

Consider in pairs or individually the following tasks as preparation for group discussion.

- How do the examples of targets here related to those you use as a department or those you use as an individual teacher?
- Are there any targets you feel are not appropriate in your context?
- How could the examples be adapted to be useful in this department?
- How could they be best collated/distributed/used?

Targets in Modern Languages

Français

- Try to speak French when and where you can in this lesson.

- Learn to read, write and think in French.

- Always write the date in full – in French.

- Underline all headings.

- Always do your homework with care – learning homework is just as important as written homework.

- Make sure you bring the correct equipment to lessons.

- Lost exercise books must be replaced at your own cost.

- No graffiti should be on or in exercise books – take pride your work.

- Use the back of exercise books (or paper) for rough work; use the front for class and homework.

Source: Coundon Court School

Targets in Modern Languages

For department use when marking, giving feedback, writing reports, and helping students complete the department review sheets. The list is not exhaustive.

Writing

- Aim for greater accuracy by copying notes carefully and correctly from the board.

- Copy accurately from the board as this forms the basis for subsequent learning.

- Use a dictionary to check if unsure of spelling.

- Check homework before handing it in with specific reference to accents/gender/ adjectives/verbs.

- [name]'s target is to keep a neat and accurate notebook.

- Can improve the presentation of his/her work by writing the headings in French and underlining them with a ruler.

- He/She must complete corrections on a regular basis and learn from his/her mistakes.

- I would like [name] to try out some of the different ways of learning vocabulary which we have discussed in class to help raise his/her test scores.

- Focus on the learning of new vocabulary. He/She has a chart to help with this at the back of his/her book – he/she could use the AQA exam guide for this.

- He/She should aim to write accurate French from memory.

- He/She should practise using the past, present and future tenses in his/her speaking and writing as these are vital for Level 5/6/a good GCSE grade.

- He/She should practise expressing her opinions and giving a reason for them.

- He/She could try producing longer sentences by including a joining word, e.g. because, where, who, etc.

- He/She could aim for greater variety in his/her writing by varying the subject of the verb, e.g. mum and I, my friends, the Spanish, etc.

- Try to vary the beginning of your sentences, e.g. then, after having, usually, etc.

- I advise him/her to use the language we practise in class as a starting point for his/her coursework.

- He/She must beware of over-using the dictionary.

Speaking

- To improve his/her pronunciation he/she must listen carefully in class repetition work and try hard to reproduce the sounds.

- He/she must work on 'sounding French'. He/She could read aloud/record him-/herself on tape at home to boost his/her confidence.

- [name] must put his/her hand up at least twice per lesson to volunteer his/her answers.

- He/She must speak up at every opportunity in order to prepare for his/her speaking exam which is worth 25% of the marks.

- He/She can only develop this skill through practice.

- Ask as well as answer questions.

- Try taking the intiative by adding another piece of information/ detail before being asked.

- He/She could practise predicting what the next question might be.

Reading and listening

- Listen for key words.

- Listen for main points and some details.

- Listen to the tone of voice to help work out opinions and feelings, do some independent reading of the simple readers and magazines in the library/Open Language Centre.

- To practise his/her listening he/she could use the interactive material which is available in our OLC.

- Extra exam-style listening practice is available using his/her copy of *Das Stimmt/Bravo/Clarísimo*.

- It is important to be able to draw conclusions from what he/she reads/hears.

- He/She needs to understand and describe feelings and emotions in Fr/Ge/Sp/Jp.

Source: Tile Hill Wood School and Language College

Appendix 1: Marking/written academic guidance in Modern Languages

Given the importance of speaking in the Modern Languages classroom, it is important to give **feedback on a student's participation,** pronunciation, willingness to enter a role, to extend her answers in class and performance in speaking tests. This may be in the form of a written comment in exercise books or a department slip issued during the course of the lesson in recognition of progress with speaking skills. Students are to stick these in their exercise books.

Books are marked regularly, **every fortnight ideally** and more regularly where possible.

Every piece of work shows evidence of being marked. This may be by the student herself (or peer) of a class reading/listening exercise, for example. Student involvement in her own marking helps her to evaluate her own work. This may be by the teacher, sometimes in the presence of the student. This is a valuable exercise as it presents the opportunity for dialogue between the teacher and the student.

Generally, every error is marked, although this may depend on the student's ability and the focus of the work, particularly in the case of Special Needs pupils. Date, title, headings are always written in the target language and checked for accuracy. Mistakes are corrected in full the first time they occur and subsequently underlined. It is best to write out the whole word containing the mistake either above the error or in the margin.

An appropriate comment is drawn from the **department bank of target language phrases.** 'Mini-posters' of these are issued to Year 7 (and again periodically as required) and are stuck at the back of exercise books.

In Years 7–9 the emphasis in the first instance is on good presentation and accurate copying of new words and phrases. A numerical mark may be appropriate for reading/listening exercises and vocabulary tests which are stuck in at the back of books. Positive comments which recognise the student's effort and personal progress are used. **Specific advice for improvement** should be given where possible. This is often appropriate with the end-of-unit activities, e.g. video, poem, survey, display work, postcard, etc. This is formative for the student, useful for our forward planning and helps familiarise students with our expectations of them. Advice may be given in the target language or English.

National Curriculum levels are indicated on unit tests and on appropriate classwork activities every half-term in line with whole-school policy. These are marked across the year group to a common mark scheme. They are retained in the class folder where teachers/students record their levels and comment on their progress. The NC sheets, which are issued to students give an overview of the level descriptors and give students targets to aim for.

In Years 9–11, marking of certain pieces of work reflects the exam requirements. Reference is made to the GCSE grade descriptors which are issued at the start of Year 10. In listening/reading marking is based on communication of understanding. If errors lead to ambiguity or failure to communicate information, marks are not awarded. In writing exercises communication and quality of language (range and accuracy) are the categories for the awarding of marks. Members of the department attend AQA speaking and coursework inset meetings. **Department standardisation of coursework** is carried out. Exemplar assignments are available for staff reference and for use with students.

It is important in both key stages that students are **familiar with the assessment criteria** before they complete important pieces of work. i.e. we explain how a written test will be marked, show how marks are awarded. It is often appropriate to give students or get them to compile a 'menu' or checklist of content points and language points to be included in a piece of speaking or writing. Familiarity with the NC level descriptors and the GCSE grade descriptors helps with this.

Time is devoted in class to the return of marked work. This may include class discussion of common errors, a class exercise where students are asked to mark themselves a compilation of mistakes made by the group, students reading comments written, completion of corrections, follow-up with individuals. Students are encouraged to **complete corrections,** at home if time is not allocated in class and to complete important pieces of unfinished work.

Marks/comments are recorded in teachers' mark books. It is helpful to differentiate between skills, classwork and homework, etc.

The marking of exercise books is monitored periodically by the HoD. There is also a yearly review of marking with a written report to the Head.

Source: Tile Hill Wood School and Language College

Appendix 2: MFL Department marking policy: code of practice

The Modern Languages marking policy is used by all teachers of French and German. The policy applies to KS3 and more broadly at KS4. At KS5 marking out of 20 or a percentage is more frequently used.

The aim of marking is to check on pupils' understanding of tasks covered in class. It should encourage independent learning and practise skills learned in the classroom. The marking system should provide feedback for the student and parents alike. Both effort and attainment are recognised. At both KS3 and KS4 these grades pertain to the ability of the group.

Homework marks/grades should be recorded by the teacher. The majority of homework set should be teacher marked, the balance being marked by students. Pupils' work should be marked on a regular basis; usually at least once per fortnight. Marking should be positive and encouraging wherever possible. Corrections should be made to pieces of written homework at the discretion of the individual teacher. Sometimes an underlining system may be used so that the pupils can evaluate their own spellings and grammar. These are clarified in a future lesson. By using this method they can recognise their own skills and highlight weaknesses. The process should enable the teacher and pupil to set individual targets, thus raising achievement.

Pupils should also spend time in addition to this on revision/learning. Thought should be given to differentiation: tasks that have outcomes according to ability; homework that becomes progressively more difficult; homeworks that are differentiated according to pupil ability.

A letter is used to indicate effort and a number to provide an attainment grade. The whole curriculum area has agreed the criteria. If a pupil achieves an A1 grade for three consecutive pieces of homework, they are duly rewarded, usually with a merit or a positive communication slip, which is also passed on to parents.

All pupils have a copy of the marking system, together with typical comments in both the target language and English. This enables parents to have a clear understanding of the marking system too. It is also displayed in the classroom for easy reference for the pupils.

Source: Coundon Court School

Appendix 3:
Mark scheme for KS3

Effort grade

A   You have made every effort to produce your best work. Well done!

B   A good effort. Your work is complete and you have taken some care.

C   An acceptable effort which could be further improved with more care and attention to detail.

D   A poor effort. You need to take more care with your work.

E   Unacceptable. You have made very little effort at all.

Achievement grade

1   An excellent piece of work.

2   A good piece of work.

3   A satisfactory piece of work.

4   An unsatisfactory piece of work.

5   A poor piece of work.

Comments

When your work is marked you will have a comment written on it. Here are some possible comments. Ask your teacher if you do not understand something.

Excellent/Génial/Chouette	Excellent/Super
Très bien	Very good
Bon travail	Good work
Bien/bien fait	Good/Well done
Assez bien	Quite good
C'est (beaucoup) mieux	It's (much) better
Bon effort	Good try/effort
Pas mal	Not bad
C'est insuffisant	Insufficient/Not enough
A refaire	To do again
Viens me voir	See me!

Correcting symbols

<u>Imediately</u>	Misspelling underlined
We legged it quick ~~~~~~~~~~~~~~	Inappropriate, out of context or unclear expression to be highlighted by a wavy line
‖	To be inserted as appropriate where a new paragraph should start
The headmasters vision	Punctuation marks to be highlighted by circling where necessary
← →	To be used where better sense would be made by moving a word in a sentence
⋏	To indicate any omission

Source: Coundon Court School

Appendix 4:
MFL assessment policy

As a department we aim to have a consistent approach to assessment and to use our assessment to inform our teaching and to increase our students' attainment. KS2 and KS3 SATs scores in Maths, English and Science are noted from the school database in our mark books and used as an **indicator of potential.** Formative assessment of day-to-day progress depends on prompt and regular **marking** of written work and **academic guidance,** which may be written or verbal on performance in speaking activities, for example. The HoD, supported by the seconds in department, are responsible for monitoring the marking of the department and we look at a sample of exercise books each term. Whilst marking must remain manageable, we aim to give at least one more detailed response to each topic with guidance on how to make further progress. A copy of the general guidelines for marking/written academic guidance in MFL, discussed and formulated by the department, is included in the handbook.

In addition to ongoing assessment in the classroom, regular written/verbal vocabulary tests are given to follow the learning homeworks which are integral to our teaching. Pupils keep any tests, stuck in at the back of exercise books and aim to improve on their scores through discussion of the **'Vocabulary learning strategies'** which were formulated with staff and students in 1997/98. All students are issued each year with the help sheet which is again to be glued at the back of books for easy reference. Please ensure that the class poster is also on display.

At KS3 each unit of work in each language is tested on completion with a selection of tests at a range of levels and on different attainment targets. The test is selected and agreed upon by the department and levels are awarded according to a common marking scheme agreed in department discussion. At the end of Year 9 all groups sit Foundation reading and listening GCSE papers.

There are implications for **schemes of work** if we are to coach the majority of our students to reach the expectations; we must ensure they are given the opportunity to **work at these higher levels** for long enough. Bearing in mind the capabilities of our groups, it is important to ensure early coverage of the tenses and then to recycle them in subsequent topics. As always we must share the level descriptors and assessment criteria with our students before they complete tasks. The publication of the QCA schemes of work for French, German and Spanish in KS3 has helped us in our planning. These documents have been used to draw up the new schemes of work.

Teacher assessment of our students' overall performance at the end of KS3 refers to a body of work produced over the year by the student. This can include levels given to classwork, homework and unit tests, as well as to performance in class. Students' work may 'show characteristics of Level ...', a student may be 'working towards Level ...' or she may have 'given evidence of performance at Level ...'. However, attainment should be sustained over a period of time. Our judgement is based on a range of pieces of work and performance in class in a variety of contexts. We need to give the most appropriate level in each skill following the 'best fit' idea, checking against adjacent levels. Performance may well be uneven across the Attainment Targets. To support us in our judgements, we have the original SCAA tapes and booklets 'Exemplification of standards' and the more recent updating on the QCA website: **www.qca.org.uk.**

Speaking tests are also a regular feature of our assessment in all key stages. Role plays, mini presentations and question/answer work may be conducted between teacher–pupil, pupil–pupil or assistant–pupil and may or may not be taped as necessary. It is helpful to make a few notes at the time of the oral on aspect such as pronunciation, communication, accuracy, etc in order to give written feedback on an individual basis to students.

At KS4 Year 10 formal exams take place in June. As in Year 9, all students take a foundation reading and listening paper with Higher papers as appropriate. The Year 11 mock exam in Dec/Jan consists of the Foundation/Higher Level past papers as appropriate. From Sept 2001 the AQA modular GCSE is to be piloted with the lowest groups in French, German and Spanish. The pattern of assessment for these groups will reflect the requirements of the new specifications.

Early familiarisation with the grade descriptors and marking criteria is essential so that students know what they are aiming for. Student progress is monitored by the class teacher, the head of department and by the head teacher, in particular, just before and after the mock examinations. The HoD sees all classes to lead a discussion 'What will make the difference?' which encompasses attitude and revision techniques leading up to the exams. Students are then involved themselves in an evaluation of their mock exam in which they identify strengths and weaknesses and set targets for further improvement. 'Expectations of our Year 11 students' which highlights the partnership between staff and students and a tick list of extra tasks to encourage independent work are issued. It is hoped these processes will help to foster independent learning and a sense of personal responsibility. Emphasis is placed on developing technique in the different skills. 'THW tips for success' are published on the intranet.

Recording

Careful recording and storing of assessment is vital **a)** to provide accurate evidence of teacher assessment at the end of the Key Stage and **b)** to inform our future planning. In addition to keeping records in our mark books, we compile a class folder with individual student records for each group at KS3/4/5. These are to be kept up to date and readily available. They are an invaluable document: it is a concise record of progress for use at parents' evenings, it allows the HoD to check on progress at times of concern, it assists the student to become involved in her own assessment and target setting and it is passed on to the subsequent teacher, following the student through the Key Stage.

The KS3 folder consists of a plastic wallet for each student which contains the following:

- the profile sheet showing attainment targets and levels achieved in each unit test with short comments on progress from student/teacher as appropriate;

- the KS3 test papers;

- a copy of the annual report sent to parents;

- any relevant special needs information e.g. reading age, IEP, etc;

- any outstanding work produced for display or using IT.

- the MFL review and target sheet conducted at the time of the whole year group progress review and/or again before reports/parents' evening (see calendar). This is a crucial process which provides students with the opportunity to reflect on the learning process, on what they need to do to improve and it opens the way for teacher dialogue with the individual student and often with parents.

Student-friendly NC level descriptors are issued to students at the start of each year and stuck in at the back of exercise books. These complement the classroom posters and allow students to see the requirements of the next level.

At KS4/5 the class folder contains:

- Year 10 exam papers and Year 11 mock papers;
- an exam evaluation sheet (see pro-forma);
- the review and target sheet;
- a copy of the annual report and, in the sixth form, progress reviews and UCAS references.

Report writing

The programme for reports and parents' evenings is published each year in the school calendar. The HoD, supported by the seconds in the department, is responsible for ensuring that teachers complete reports in accordance with school guidelines. Reports should be passed to the HoD the week before they are due with tutors. Please refer to 'Guidance on report writing' in your THW Development Planner. We must give 1 or 2 NC levels at KS3 and in Year 10 a GCSE grade or one within a range of three and in Year 11 a GCSE grade or one within a range of two. We must refer to achievement in the four attainment targets as specified in the 'Area for Comment'. We should aim to describe strengths and weaknesses, giving specific advice on how to make progress. A useful bank of department targets has been compiled for use in report writing and progress reviews and is attached. As a department we have also decided to comment on specific pieces of outstanding work, whether in terms of effort and/or achievement, thorough learning of vocabulary, a good response in oral work, particular effort with research or completion of homework, helpfulness in class, an improvement in attitude, etc.

Rewarding achievement

In addition to regular, positive praise to students of their work, there is a school rewards system of commendations which are to be awarded for particular effort/achievement. Students record these at the back of their study planners and we are to sign and date them. In addition we use a variety of stickers and stamps as reward and encouragement. Girls should be sent to the HoD for recognition of outstanding work/effort. Department stickers have been designed to reward outstanding oral contribution.

Source: Tile Hill Wood School and Language College

Appendix 5: Pupil-friendly level descriptions

PROGRESS THROUGH THE LEVELS:
As a Year 7/8/9 Modern Languages Pupil you can ...

Attainment Target	Level 1	Level 2	Level 3	Level 4	Level 5	Level 6	Level 7
1 Listening and Responding	▪ Understand instructions, questions and short phrases with the help of repetition, mime or pictures	▪ Understand a range of phrases, sentences & instructions in language already met, with some repetition ▪ Respond, using words or actions	▪ Understand with repetition a series of phrases. e.g. using known language, short messages, conversations, instructions spoken at near normal speed ▪ Note main points and details	▪ Understand longer passages using familiar language in simple sentences from one topic ▪ Some repetition needed	▪ Understand familiar language from several topic areas at near normal speed ▪ Understand when present and past or future events are described	▪ Understand familiar language in new situations covering past, present ± future events with little repetition at normal speed, e.g. story or description of an event	▪ Understand passages which contain longer sentences and some new language, rarely needing repetition, e.g. news items from TV/radio
2 Speaking	▪ Use single words/short phrases when speaking ▪ Need repetition to practise correct pronunciation ▪ Need some picture clues for help	▪ Use short set phrases/sentences ▪ Ask for permission or help in the classroom ▪ Say things clearly but still need pronunciation practise	▪ Take part in short conversations of 2–3 exchanges with prompts ▪ Use mostly learnt language ▪ Change a few words	▪ Take part in a short conversation of 3–4 exchanges using prompts ▪ Use grammar to adapt some words + phrases	▪ Take part in a short conversation using present and past or future tenses ▪ Give and ask for information + opinions	▪ Use the past, present and future tenses ▪ Use grammar to build your own phrases in new contexts ▪ Make yourself understood fairly easily	▪ Take the lead in + develop a conversation on things of personal and topical interest ▪ Adapt language to say things in different ways ▪ Sound like a native speaker
3 Reading and Responding	▪ Understand clearly written single words, often with the help of a picture	▪ Understand short words + phrases seen before ▪ Read aloud familiar words + phrases ▪ Look up the meaning of new words in book/glossary	▪ Understand short printed texts containing familiar language ▪ Note main points ▪ Use a dictionary/glossary ▪ Choose something to read on your own	▪ Understand short, printed and hand-written texts ▪ Note main points and some details ▪ Read alone using a dictionary/glossary or working out what words mean	▪ Understand on your own a variety of texts, e.g. leaflets, articles with present and past or future events in them	▪ Understand a variety of texts with past and present and future tenses using familiar language in new situations ▪ Scan a selection of written material and choose something which interests you to read on your own ▪ Use clues more confidently to work out meaning	▪ Understand imaginative and factual material containing some language not met before ▪ Use language met in reading materials in your s/w ▪ Use reference materials
4 Writing	▪ Copy words you know correctly ▪ Label pictures and choose the right word to fill in gaps in short sentences	▪ Copy short phrases you know correctly ▪ Spell words from memory usually well enough to be understood	▪ Write with support 2–3 sentences on familiar topics ▪ Express likes/dislikes ▪ Write short phrases from memory ▪ Use understandable spelling	▪ Write a paragraph of 3–4 sentences, using memorised language ▪ Begin to use grammar to add/change single words/phrases ▪ Use a dictionary to check	▪ Write a short piece in simple sentences ▪ Refer to past experiences or future plans as well as things you do every day	▪ Write in paragraphs, referring to past, present and future events ▪ Use knowledge of grammar to make up new sentences	▪ Write on real and imaginary subjects ▪ Link sentences and structure ideas ▪ Redraft your work to improve quality

Source: Tile Hill Wood School and Language College

PROGRESS THROUGH THE LEVELS:
As a Year 7 Modern Languages Pupil you can …

Attainment Target	Level 1	Level 2	Level 3	Level 4
1 Listening and Responding	▪ Understand instructions, questions and short phrases with the help of repetition, mime or pictures	▪ Understand a range of phrases, sentences & instructions in language already met, with some repetition ▪ Respond, using words or actions	▪ Understand with repetition a series of phrases, e.g. using known language, short messages, conversations, instructions spoken at near normal speed ▪ Note main points and details	▪ Understand longer passages using familiar language in simple sentences from <u>one</u> topic ▪ Some repetition needed
2 Speaking	▪ Use single words/short phrases when speaking ▪ Need repetition to practise correct pronunciation ▪ Need some picture clues for help	▪ Use short set phrases/sentences ▪ Ask for permission or help in the classroom ▪ Say things clearly but still need pronunciation practise	▪ Take part in short conversations of 2–3 exchanges with prompts ▪ Use mostly learnt language ▪ Change a few words	▪ Take part in a short conversation of 3–4 exchanges using prompts ▪ Use grammar to adapt some words + phrases
3 Reading and Responding	▪ Understand clearly written single words, often with the help of a picture	▪ Understand short words + phrases seen before ▪ Read aloud familiar words + phrases ▪ Look up the meaning of new words in book/glossary	▪ Understand short printed texts containing <u>familiar</u> language ▪ Note main points ▪ Use a dictionary/glossary ▪ Choose something to read on your own	▪ Understand short, printed <u>and</u> hand-written texts ▪ Note main points and some details ▪ Read alone using a dictionary/glossary or working out what words mean
4 Writing	▪ Copy words you know correctly ▪ Label pictures and choose the right word to fill in gaps in short sentences	▪ Copy short phrases you know correctly ▪ Spell words from memory usually well enough to be understood	▪ Write <u>with</u> support 2–3 sentences on familiar topics ▪ Express likes/dislikes ▪ Write short phrases from memory ▪ Use understandable spelling	▪ Write a paragraph of 3–4 sentences, using memorised language ▪ Begin to use grammar to add/change single words/phrases ▪ Use a dictionary to check

Source: Tile Hill Wood School and Language College

PROGRESS THROUGH THE LEVELS:
As a Year 8/9 Modern Languages Pupil you can ...

Attainment Target	Level 3	Level 4	Level 5	Level 6	Level 7
1 Listening and Responding	• Understand with repetition a series of phrases, e.g. using known language, short messages, conversations, instructions spoken at near normal speed • Note main points and details	• Understand longer passages using familiar language in simple sentences from one topic • Some repetition needed	• Understand familiar language from several topic areas at near normal speed • Understand when present and past or future events are described	• Understand familiar language in new situations covering past, present ± future events with little repetition at normal speed, e.g. story or description of an event	• Understand passages which contain longer sentences and some new language, rarely needing repetition, e.g. news items from TV/radio
2 Speaking	• Take part in short conversations of 2–3 exchanges with prompts • Use mostly learnt language • Change a few words	• Take part in a short conversation of 3–4 exchanges using prompts • Use grammar to adapt some words + phrases	• Take part in a short conversation using present and past or future tenses • Give and ask for information + opinions	• Use the past, present and future tenses • Use grammar to build your own phrases in new contexts • Make yourself understood fairly easily	• Take the lead in + develop a conversation on things of personal and topical interest • Adapt language to say things in different ways • Sound like a native speaker
3 Reading and Responding	• Understand short printed texts containing familiar language • Note main points • Use a dictionary/glossary • Choose something to read on your own	• Understand short, printed and hand-written texts • Note main points and some details • Read alone using a dictionary/glossary or working out what words mean	• Understand on your own a variety of texts eg leaflets, articles with present and past or future events in them	• Understand a variety of texts with past and present and future tenses using familiar language in new situations • Scan a selection of written material and choose something which interests you to read on your own • Use clues more confidently to work out meaning	• Understand imaginative and factual material containing some language not met before • Use language met in reading materials in your s/w • Use reference materials
4 Writing	• Write with support 2–3 sentences on familiar topics • Express likes/dislikes • Write short phrases from memory • Use understandable spelling	• Write a paragraph of 3–4 sentences, using memorised language • Begin to use grammar to add/change single words/phrases • Use a dictionary to check	• Write a short piece in simple sentences • Refer to past experiences or future plans as well as things you do every day	• Write in paragraphs, referring to past, present and future events • Use knowledge of grammar to make up new sentences	• Write on real and imaginary subjects • Link sentences and structure ideas • Redraft your work to improve quality

Source: Tile Hill Wood School and Language College

Appendix 5

References and
further reading

Adams, J. (2002) *Languages for real purposes.* Folens.

Assessment Reform Group (2002) *Assessment for Learning.* **www.assessment-reform-group.org.uk** (accessed 10.12.02).

Barnes, A. (1999) 'Assessment'. In Pachler, N. and Field, K. (eds) *Teaching Modern Languages at advanced level:* 251–281. Routledge.

Barnes, A. and Graham, S. (1997) *Concepts 11: Target language testing.* Mary Glasgow Publications/ ALL.

Black, P. and Wiliam, D. (1998), 'Inside the black box: raising standards through classroom assessment'. In: *Phi Delta Kappan,* Volume 10 (see **www.pdkintl.org/ kappan/kbla9810.htm,** accessed 20.6.02, and **www.kcl.ac.uk/depsta/education/ publications/blackbox.html**).

Black, P., Harrison, C., Lee, C., Marshall, B., and Wiliam, D. (2002) *Working inside the black box: assessment for learning in the classroom.* Department of Education and Professional Studies, King's College.

Blum, R. (1984) *Effective schooling practices: a research synthesis.* Portland, Oregon: Northwest Regional Educational Laboratory.

Brew, A. (1999) 'Towards autonomous assessment: using self-assessment and peer-assessment'. In: Brown, S. and Glasner, A. (eds) *Assessment matters in higher education:* 159–171. SRHE and Open University Press.

Broadfoot, P. (2000) 'Assessment and intuition'. In: Atkinson, T. and Claxton, G. *The intuitive practitioner: on the value of not always knowing what one is doing:* 199–219. Open University Press.

Brooks, V. (2002) *Assessment in secondary schools: the new teacher's guide to monitoring, assessment, recording, reporting and accountability.* Open University Press.

Carter, D. (2003) New Pathfinder 2: *The language of success: improving grades at GCSE.* CILT.

Common European Framework of Reference for Languages: learning, teaching and assessment. Cambridge University Press, 2001.

DfEE (2000) *Hay McBer Report: research into teacher effectiveness.* **www.teachernet.gov.uk/ Education_Overview/strategy/haymcber** (accessed 26.11.02).

DfES (2002) *Languages for all: languages for life. A strategy for England.* DfES Publications.

Dickinson, L. (1987) *Self-instruction in language learning.* Cambridge University Press.

Dobson, A. (1998) *MFL inspected: reflections on inspection findings 1996/7.* CILT.

Dobson, A. (2000) 'European Language Portfolio'. In: Byram, M. (ed) *Encyclopaedia of language teaching and learning: 204–6.* Routledge.

Dobson, A. (2002) 'An update on HMI findings'. In: *MFL* Issue 1. CILT.

Downes, P. and Mitchell, I. (2000) *TES MFL Curriculum Special* (Spring 2000). *TES.*

Gipps, C. (1994) *Beyond testing – towards a theory of educational assessment.* The Falmer Press.

Graham, S. (1997) *Effective language learning.* Multilingual Matters.

Grenfell, M. and Harris, V. (1999) *Modern Languages and learning strategies: in theory and practice.* Routledge.

Harris, V. (1997) Pathfinder 31: *Teaching learners how to learn: strategy training in the Modern Languages classroom.* CILT.

Harris, V. (2002), 'Treading a tightrope. Supporting boys to achieve in MFL'. In: Swarbrick, A. (ed) *Teaching Modern Foreign Languages in secondary schools: a reader: 187–202.* Routledge Falmer.

Hunt, M. (2001) 'Principles and theoretical approaches in assessment' and 'Checking on progress: developing approaches to giving formal and informal feedback' in Arthur, L. and Hurd, S. (eds) *Supporting lifelong language learning.* Open University/CILT.

Macaro, E. (1997) *Target language, collaborative learning and autonomy.* Multilingual Matters.

Macaro, E. (2001) *Learning strategies in foreign and second language classrooms.* Continuum.

National Curriculum Council (1992) *Modern Foreign Languages: non-statutory guidance for England and Wales.* National Curriculum Council.

Nicholls, G. (1999) *Learning to teach: a handbook for primary and secondary school teachers.* Kogan Page.

OFSTED (1995) *Modern Foreign Languages: a review of inspection findings 1993/4.* HMSO.

OFSTED (1996) *Subjects and standards: issues for school development arising from OFSTED inspection findings 1994–5: Key Stages 3 and 4 and post-16.* HMSO.

OFSTED (1999) *Inspecting subjects and aspects 11–18: Modern Foreign Languages.* HMSO.

OFSTED (1999) *Modern Foreign Languages: a review of inspection findings 1997/8.* HMSO.

OFSTED (2002a) *Good teaching, effective departments: Findings from an HMI survey of subject teaching in secondary schools 2000/2001* (available at **www.ofsted.gov.uk**).

OFSTED (2002b) *Secondary subject reports 2000/2001* (available at **www.ofsted.gov.uk**).

Pachler, N. and Field, K. (2001) *Learning to teach Modern Foreign Languages in the secondary school, a companion to school experience.* 2nd ed. Routledge.

Parr, H. (1997) Pathfinder 29: *Assessment and planning in the MFL department.* CILT.

QCA, DfES (1999) *Modern Foreign Languages. The National Curriculum for England.* HMSO.

Richards, J. (1998) *Beyond training.* Cambridge University Press.

Richards, J. and Lockhart, C. (1994) *Reflective teaching in second language classrooms.* Cambridge University Press.

SCAA (1996) *MFL: Consistency in teacher assessment. Exemplification of standards: Key Stage 3.* SCAA.

SCAA (1996, 1997) *Modern Foreign Languages – optional tests and tasks* (French, Spanish, German, Urdu plus Teacher's Handbook). SCAA.

Stiggins, R. (2002) 'Assessment crisis: the absence of assessment for learning'. In: *Phi Delta Kappan*, Vol. 83, No. 10: 758–765.

Stobart, G. and Gipps, C. (1997) *Assessment: a teacher's guide to the issues.* 3rd ed. Hodder & Stoughton.

Teacher Training Agency (2002) *Qualifying to teach: standards for the award of Qualified Teacher Status* (available at **www.canteach.gov.uk**).

Vandergrift, L. (1999) 'Facilitating second language listening comprehension: acquiring successful strategies'. In: *English Language Teaching Journal.*

Weeden, P., Winter, J. and Broadfoot, P. (2002) *Assessment. What's in it for schools?* Routledge/Falmer.

Wiliam, D. and Black, P. (2002) 'Feedback is the best nourishment'. In: *Times Educational Supplement*, 4.10.02: 8 of 'Mind Measuring' supplement. *TES.*

Williams, J. (1999) 'An introduction to teaching'. In: Nicholls, G. *Learning to teach. A handbook for primary and secondary school teachers:* 3–15. Kogan Page.

Williams, M. and Burden, R. (1997) *Psychology for language teachers: a social constructivist approach.* Cambridge University Press.

Useful websites

General assessment advice

Guidance on assessment and evaluation is available at: **www.teachernet.gov.uk/ Assessment_and_evaluation.**

Using ICT in assessment

ICT is an area which can also be considered **a)** to streamline some assessment procedures/data collection and analysis, and **b)** where MARRA has particular characteristics to take account of the different possibilities of ICT and the potential emphasis on IT rather than language. Terry Atkinson has produced a very good module on Graham Davies' ICT4LT site. Please see **www.ict4lt.org/en/en_mod4-1.htm.**

At the ICT4LT website at **www.ict4lt.org/en/en_mod4-1.htm**, there is help with electronic mark sheets and you can also download an Excel file to experiment with:

Target setting

The Standards website at **www.standards.dfes.gov.uk/ts/** gives guidance on target setting and school improvement. The following website is provided by the *Times Educational Supplement*: **www.tes.co.uk/online/made_to_measure2/target_ setting/introduction.asp.**

'Autumn package' site

www.standards.dfes.gov.uk/performance

MIDYIS, YELLIS information systems

These information systems are provided by the Curriculum, Evaluation and Management Centre at the University of Durham (**http://cem.dur.ac.uk**).

QCA assessment for learning site

www.qca.org.uk/ca/5-14/afl/?fp_clk

Assessment Reform Group

Various useful information on assessment for learning can be downloaded from **www.assessment-reform-group.org.uk** (accessed 10.12.02).